TAX WISE MONEY STRATEGIES

TAX WISE MONEY STRATEGIES

Protect Yourself from the Highest Taxes in History

Robert C. Carlson

Carroll & Graf Publishers, Inc.
New York

Copyright © 1995 by Robert C. Carlson

First Carroll & Graf edition 1995

Carroll & Graf Publishers, Inc.
260 Fifth Avenue
New York, NY 10001

Library of Congress Cataloging-in-Publication Data

Carlson, Robert C., 1957–
    Tax wise money strategies : protect yourself from the highest
taxes in history / Robert C. Carlson. — 1st Carroll & Graf ed.
        p.   cm.
    ISBN 0-7867-0165-X : $14.95
    1. Income tax—United States. 2. Finance, Personal. I. Title.
HJ4652.C286   1995
343.7305'2—dc20
[347.30352]   94-28664
                                                                CIP

Manufactured in the United States of America

Contents

TAX WISE MONEY STRATEGIES

Introduction: Using Tax Wise Money Strategies to Increase Wealth

Taxes can make you rich.

Most people view taxes as a burden they want to think about as little as possible. That is why many people overpay their taxes. But every burden has a hidden benefit, including taxes.

Taxes probably are your biggest expense (see Chapter 1 if you don't believe this). And it is easier to increase wealth by saving money or cutting expenses than by earning more money. If you earn another dollar, 40 or 50 cents of it will go to the government in taxes. But if you save a dollar, you keep the whole dollar. In addition, most people are not in a position to increase their earnings. So you should focus at least as much on keeping what you have earned as you do on earning more.

As your biggest expense, taxes also are your biggest source of potential savings and the greatest opportunity to increase your wealth.

Tax wise money strategies not only are your most accessible source of wealth, they also are a low-risk way to increase wealth. You do not have to take on a lot of debt or quit your job to start a risky business venture. The tax code is filled with provisions designed to save you thousands of dollars. All you have to do is take advantage of these opportunities.

Saving taxes is only the first step in using the tax code to increase your wealth. Your savings should be invested in tax wise ways. That way your savings compound and earn tax-sheltered returns. Your tax savings plus their tax-advantaged investment growth will build you a comfortable nest egg. Taxes take 30 percent to 50 percent of every dollar you earn.

If you can keep a fraction of that and put it to work earning more after-tax money, then you have established a low-risk system for increasing wealth.

What is a Tax Wise Money Strategy?

This book is not another tax return manual. There already are too many thick books that tell you which numbers to put on each line of your tax return. Those books don't recognize that tax saving is a year-'round activity. If you need to know how to report an item on your tax return, whether or not to claim someone as a dependent, or what filing status to use, you won't find the answers in this book. Save your money and order free publications from the IRS by calling 1-800-TAX-FORM.

This also is not one of the books that describes all the provisions of the tax code. Those books don't recognize that not all tax reduction strategies are tax wise money strategies. Every tax reduction strategy comes with a cost. Sometimes there are fees and expenses; sometimes there are restrictions on what you can do with your money. You don't want a tax strategy that ends up costing more than it saves.

Most tax books tell you when you can use a tax strategy. I tell you when it makes sense to use it—when a tax reduction strategy becomes a tax wise money strategy.

For example, you can earn tax-exempt income with tax-exempt bonds, defer investment income with variable annuities, and reduce taxes with the credit for low-income housing investments. But those other tax books won't tell you when it makes sense to invest in tax-exempt bonds and what the best way is to invest in the bonds. And they won't tell you how to select a variable annuity, which taxpayers should avoid variable annuities, and what the pitfalls are in low-income housing credits.

My goal in formulating tax wise money strategies is not simply to decrease taxes. My goal is also to use the tax code to increase after-tax wealth. A tax reduction scheme that is loaded with fees, restrictions, high investment risk, and other costs might be worse than simply paying taxes and keeping what's left over.

I give you more than the dry tax rules. I present the full picture and, using original research that goes beyond the tax code, focus on building your after-tax wealth, not just cutting taxes regardless of the other costs.

A tax wise money strategy also is a problem-solving strategy. I write about specific problems, opportunities, and major life decisions and show how to use the tax code in those situations. I also describe how to use two or more tax strategies together to boost your benefits, even when the strategies are from different parts of the tax code.

Don't Fear Tax Wise Wealth

Many people don't use the tax code to build wealth, because they fear the IRS. People fear the IRS so much that they overpay their taxes with the hope of avoiding problems with the IRS. Each year, when the IRS reports the previous year's audit activity, the statistics show that about 5 percent of audits resulted in *net refunds* to the audited taxpayers, with an average refund of $1,500. If you extrapolate that to all taxpayers, Americans collectively overpay about $23 billion in federal income taxes.

But if 5 percent of audits result in net refunds, obviously overpaying your taxes will not help you avoid an audit.

You reduce the risk of an audit by using tax reduction strategies that the IRS and Congress accept. The strategies in this book are time-tested and IRS-approved. Thousands of wealthy Americans use these strategies every day because they have high-priced lawyers and accountants to explain the tax code to them. The more than one hundred thousand happy readers of my newsletter *Tax Wise Money* also are benefiting from these strategies without fear of the IRS.

I wrote this book in the same concise, easy-to-read style that makes my newsletter useful to so many readers. You won't find extra words or long quotes from that monument to functional illiteracy known as the Internal Revenue Code. This book is more of a Cliff Notes for the tax code. You get all the important, practical information in a usable format.

It is much easier to build wealth by saving money than by earning more money. If your ultimate goal is to increase after-tax wealth, this book is for you. You will learn practical, commonsense strategies that make the consistent growth of after-tax wealth inevitable.

Chapter 1

Treasure in the Tax Code

On February 15, 1993, millions of Americans sat in front of their television sets and watched President Bill Clinton break his campaign promises. There would be no middle-class tax cut, no reduction in capital gains taxes, no reduction in Social Security payroll taxes, and no reinstatement of IRA deductions. Instead, we would get the highest tax increase in U.S. history, including:

- higher individual income taxes, with the top rate rising to 39.6 percent;
- even higher effective tax rates for upper-income individuals because various tax benefits are reduced or phased out as income rises;
- higher taxes on corporations and businesses;
- much higher taxes on many retirees;
- the strong possibility of ever higher taxes in the future.

The president referred to the new taxes as only "a good beginning" and talked openly of possible new taxes: a value-added tax or national sales tax, even higher tax rates, and a reduction of the mortgage interest deduction.

The More Things Change ...

Americans are used to presidents breaking their campaign promises, particularly on taxes. For example, an ad campaign for a mutual fund company specializing in tax-exempt bonds displays photographs of six presidents from Calvin Coolidge to George Bush. Beneath each photograph is a quote from that president promising either lower taxes or tax reform.

The point is clear: American politicians running for office promise lower taxes but never deliver.

Taxes Are Your Biggest Expense

You pay federal income taxes, Social Security taxes, and Medicare taxes. You also pay state income or property taxes or both. And you pay a number of hidden taxes, such as sales taxes and excise taxes. Higher taxes are the primary reason that the younger generations of Americans don't believe they will live as well as their parents have.

You spend a big part of the year working to pay taxes. Each year the Tax Foundation of Washington, D.C., calculates how long the average American works just to pay federal and state taxes. In 1993, the average taxpayer worked until May 3 to pay his or her taxes. The money earned for the rest of the year was available to pay for food, housing, clothing, and other necessities. In a high tax state, Tax Freedom Day came even later. Residents of New York and Washington, D.C., worked until May 22 to pay their taxes, while Tax Freedom Day was April 25 for residents of Virginia.

The Tax Foundation also estimates how much of the average workday is devoted to paying taxes. In 1993, out of each eight-hour day, the average American worked one hour, forty-three minutes to pay federal taxes, and another fifty-nine minutes to pay state and local taxes.

Treasure in the Tax Code

That's enough bad news. The good news is that you actually can use the tax code to increase your wealth and build your fortune. Do not buy into the myth that tax reform took away all the good tax strategies.

You saw some prime examples of how to use the tax code to build wealth during the 1992 presidential campaign. Billionaire Ross Perot paid an effective tax rate of about 4 percent on his income. He did this by investing and spending in ways that cut his taxes while increasing his assets. President George Bush was able to pay no state income taxes by claiming Texas as his residence, though he spent most of his time in Washington, D.C., and Maine. Bill and Hillary Clinton saved taxes by, among other things, donating old underwear to charity.

Anyone can use the tax code to build wealth. All you need is information. Tax reduction is not only for the rich, and you do not need expensive financial pros to help you find treasure in the tax code.

How Taxes Can Make You Rich

Suppose you could save $2,000 in taxes each year and invest that savings in the long term. After five years you have saved $10,000, and after ten years you have saved $20,000. But there is more. Instead of spending your tax savings, you invest it. Your tax savings can earn you more money, and investing the savings in tax wise ways compounds your returns.

Suppose you can earn a 10 percent average annual return on your investments before taxes. If you invest in a fully taxable account and are in a combined federal and state income tax bracket of 35 percent, you earn only 6.5 percent after taxes. After ten years your investment fund has grown to about $26,989 after taxes, for a net profit of $6,989. After twenty years you would have $77,650.

A better solution is to make tax wise investments. Look for ways to earn your 10 percent tax-free or tax-deferred.

If you could keep the entire 10 percent return on your investment, you would have $31,875 after ten years and $114,455 after twenty years. That is a significant difference, or, as they say in Washington, we're starting to talk about real money. You end up with about 18 percent more money after ten years because you learned tax wise ways to invest.

You say that it is not possible to achieve these kinds of tax savings anymore? I will show you many ways in this book to earn tax-free and tax-deferred investment income. I also will show you how to shelter your investment income from taxes through deductions and other methods.

A Tale of Two Families

Meet the Joneses and the Johnsons. They live next door to each other, and Mr. Jones and Mr. Johnson work for the same company. Each makes about $75,000 annually and has a mortgage of about $75,000 on homes valued at about $200,000. Both Mrs. Jones and Mrs. Johnson work part time, and each makes about $5,000 annually. Each family has two children.

To all outside appearances the families are nearly identical. They have lived next door to each other for more than a decade, and the two husbands

Chart 1
Tax Wise Wealth Building
How Tax Savings Grow

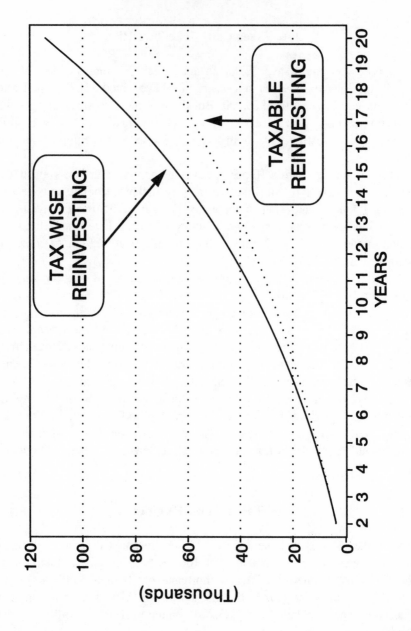

have been working together even longer. But things are different when you look closer.

The Johnsons are concerned about their financial situation. They do not seem to be saving any money. Their net worth consists almost entirely of their home equity, some money in a bank account, and IRAs to which they have not contributed for several years. They wonder how they will be able to send the children to college, pay off their debts, and save enough money for a comfortable retirement.

In the Jones household, the situation is entirely different. That's because the Joneses started using tax wise money strategies years ago.

For years, Mr. Jones has been bringing home a bigger after-tax paycheck than Mr. Johnson. How could that be when they earn the same salary and have the same number of dependents? Simple. Mr. Jones decided he was not going to make an interest-free loan to the government each year and wait until the following spring to get a big refund. Instead, he reduced the amount of withholding that is taken from his paycheck.

Mr. Jones also did some smart things with his money that you will learn about in this book. He contributed the maximum amount he could afford to his company's 401(k) plan. The money avoided income taxes, and the income on his 401(k) account compounds tax-deferred. Better yet, his company matches Mr. Jones' 401(k) contribution with 50 cents for every dollar he contributes. Where else can you get a 50 percent risk-free return on a tax-advantaged investment?

This was just one of many benefit programs that Mr. Jones took full advantage of.

Also, Mr. Jones did not stick his savings in a taxable, low-yielding bank account the way Mr. Johnson did. Instead, Mr. Jones sought out safe, high-return, tax-advantaged investments. He contributed money to an IRA each year, even when the contribution was not deductible. You'll learn why later in the book. He also put money in a number of tax-free and tax-deferred investments. The tax savings did not seem like much at first. But over the years the magic of tax-advantaged compounding produced results. The Joneses feel confident that they are on the way to a secure retirement, and they have extra spending money available when it is needed.

Mr. Jones also looked after his children's education. He put some of his savings into investment accounts in their names. Why pay taxes on investment income at his tax rate when the children could earn it and pay little or no tax? Again, the savings did not seem like much when the kids were toddlers, but now this simple arrangement is saving the family a tidy sum in taxes each year. As the sums in his children's accounts grew, Mr. Jones had to take steps to avoid the "kiddie tax," which would have calculated some of the tax at his tax rate instead of his children's rates. Mr. Jones also learned other tricks about saving for a college education.

Meanwhile, Mrs. Jones was also practicing tax wise wealth strategies. Mrs. Johnson next door works at a local bank. She gets a salary from which income and Social Security taxes are withheld. The bank offers few employee benefits, and Mrs. Johnson cannot deduct any expenses. But Mrs. Jones has been running a small catering business from her house. The Joneses are able to deduct a portion of the home that is used exclusively for the business. When things get busy, she gets the kids to help out and pays them salaries. She deducts the salaries from her income, the children can earn up to $3,800 tax-free each year, and there are no Social Security taxes until the children are age eighteen. Mrs. Jones is able to keep more of her $5,000 after taxes than Mrs. Johnson is, and is able to keep additional money in the family. If business continues to pick up, Mrs. Jones might incorporate the catering business and get even bigger tax savings.

The Joneses pay $5,000 less in taxes each year than the Johnsons. The savings will become larger as their investment portfolio and assets grow. But if they save only $5,000 off their tax bill each year for the next twenty years and invest that to return only 5 percent after taxes, they will have $165,000 in extra wealth. Mr. Jones intends to use that money to buy a vacation home, which will again increase his annual tax savings.

Six Simple Steps to Tax Wealth

After you slice through all the jargon in the tax code, you find that no matter who you are or how much you earn, there are six major ways to pay less taxes.

• **Earn tax-free income.** Obviously if income is tax-free, you do not pay taxes on it. Some income is free of all taxes. Some is exempt from income taxes but subject to Social Security and Medicare taxes. On other income, the reverse is true. The best-known source of tax-free income is a tax-exempt bond issued by a state or local government (or a mutual fund that owns these bonds). There are many other sources of exempt income. An often-overlooked area is the benefit package offered by your employer. Many employees do not use the options they are given. As a result, they effectively are giving away a paycheck or two each year.

• **Shift income.** When someone in the 36 percent bracket earns $1,000 of interest each year, he or she keeps only $640 after federal taxes. A good move is to shift the income to a child who will pay only 15 percent or perhaps no income tax. That is the essence of income shifting. You keep income in the family and reduce the tax burden. The result is higher family wealth. The Clinton tax code makes income shifting more attractive than it has been since 1986. Business owners might be able to shift income between themselves and their corporations. Some people use trusts to shift income.

• **Defer taxes.** When you defer taxes, they are paid at some point in the future. If you can defer taxes on income and invest that income, you will benefit from tax-deferred compounding. Even if the income is later taxed at a higher rate, you are better off by deferring the taxes.

• **Generate deductions.** The best deductions are those that reduce gross income. These include business losses, capital losses, and farm losses. A major benefit of business and farm deductions is that they reduce both the self-employment tax and the income tax.

There also are deductions from gross income, including alimony payments, IRA contributions, Keogh contributions, and half of the self-employment tax.

Another category of deductions is itemized deductions, including medical expenses, state and local taxes, interest paid, charitable contributions, moving expenses, and miscellaneous expenses.

• **Take tax credits.** A tax credit is a direct dollar-for-dollar reduction in your tax. The most useful credits are those for child and dependent care and for low-income housing investments.

• **Earn capital gains.** Long-term capital gains have a top tax rate of 28 percent, while ordinary income tax rates are as high as 39.6 percent. The ordinary income tax rate is higher for some taxpayers because high-income taxpayers have their itemized deductions and dependent exemptions reduced. In the top tax bracket long-term capital gains face only 70 percent of the tax burden of ordinary income. An even lower tax rate is available for capital gains on certain small business investments or on capital gains that are reinvested in certain types of small businesses.

Capital assets also benefit from tax-deferred compounding of gains. Though a capital asset might appreciate each year, you can let the gains compound and pay taxes only when the asset is sold.

These are the only six strategies for reducing taxes. If you learn these strategies you an use them in many different ways to increase your wealth.

Beware the Second Tax

The United States actually has two tax systems: the regular income tax and the alternative minimum tax. The AMT, as it is known, is designed to keep you from eliminating income taxes by using too many tax breaks designated as "tax preferences and adjustments." Overuse these tax strategies and you will end up owing a lot of money under the AMT. Throughout this book, I include "AMT Alerts" whenever I describe a strategy that will trigger the AMT if it is overused or used with other tax preferences and adjustments. For more details on the AMT, ask for the IRS publication 909, *Alternative Minimum Tax,* and Form 6251 with instructions.

After-Tax Wealth Is What Counts

There is an old saying among tax advisers that you should not let the tax tail wag the dog. That means that you should take a tax break only when it makes financial sense. You should not take an opportunity to reduce taxes just to be reducing taxes.

For example, many people poured money into tax shelters in the late 1970s and 1980s without regard to whether the underlying investments made any sense. They wanted the tax breaks. So they invested in real estate, railroad boxcars, coal mines, oil wells, and other assets that provided great tax breaks. The problem was that many of these investments made no business sense. The investors ended up paying more to creditors of the tax shelters than they would have paid in taxes.

A tax wise money strategy does more than cut taxes. A tax wise money strategy builds after-tax wealth. And that should be the goal of your tax planning: to build after-tax wealth. You need to use the tax strategies described in this book, but only those strategies that are appropriate for you.

My goals are to show you which strategies increase after-tax wealth and to steer you away from "tax reduction" strategies that actually cost you more than they save. You need to avoid the pitfalls of tax strategies that come loaded with high expenses or that make no nontax sense. That is just as important as avoiding high taxes.

Tax wise money strategy. What's the best way to get started? Surveys show that what people hate most about taxes is pulling all their records together. I've known many people who don't take advantage of tax reduction strategies because it is too much trouble to get all their records together to see which methods make sense. You can avoid these problems by purchasing a computer and one of the personal accounting or checkbook computer programs. When you use these programs, all of your financial data will be recorded in the computer, and you can get an updated financial report within a few minutes. Using this modern technology is a great way to beat the IRS and use the tax code to build your wealth.

You generally control how much you pay in taxes. The sooner you start using tax wise money strategies, the faster you will build after-tax wealth, because the tax code can make you rich. Now let's start examining tax wise money strategies that will help make your family financially independent.

Chapter 2

Off-the-Books Income:
Earning Tax-Free Income Legally

Getting a raise or a higher-paying job is not the best way to increase after-tax wealth. Look at what happens when your salary increases:

Example. You receive a $1,000 raise on top of your $55,000 salary. Of that $1,000, a 6.2 percent goes to Social Security taxes, 1.45 percent to Medicare/Medicaid taxes (your employer matches both those payments), and 28 percent to federal income taxes. You might pay another 5 percent or so in state income taxes. You will keep roughly $600.

You increase after-tax wealth faster by keeping 100 percent of pay increases. To do that, forget about cash and ask your employer to pay your personal expenses through IRS-approved benefit programs. In fact, it can pay to take a salary *cut* in exchange for tax-exempt benefits.

Tax wise money strategy. Search for opportunities to have your employer provide tax-free benefits instead of salary increases. Most benefits avoid both income and payroll taxes. If you own a corporation, tax-free benefits work equally well for you and your employees.

There are numerous IRS-approved tax free benefits available. In this chapter I provide a checklist of benefits and tell you how to take maximum advantage of the most important ones.

Do-It-Yourself Health Care Reform

Health and accident benefits paid by an employer are tax-free as long as the benefit program does not discriminate in favor of highly compensated employees, officers, and shareholders. Get all the tax-free medical benefits you can from your employer, because you can deduct only medical expenses that exceed 7.5 percent of adjusted gross income.

Employers that do not have health plans already should consider establishing these two types:

Medical expense reimbursement plans. There are a couple of medical expense reimbursement plans.

An employer that feels it cannot afford to pay for health insurance can help employees by setting up a medical expense reimbursement plan, also known as a flexible spending account. Under these plans, employees decide how much salary to defer into medical expense accounts; that amount is automatically withheld from their paychecks, and it is not taxed. As health insurance premiums are paid and other medical and dental expenses are incurred, the employee presents receipts to the employer and gets reimbursed from the account. The reimbursements are tax-free. After-tax personal expenses have been converted into tax-free benefits.

Example. In the 28 percent income tax bracket, you have to earn $156.25 to have enough after income and payroll taxes to pay $100 of medical expenses. In the 31 percent bracket you have to earn $163.93 to have $100 after taxes. With a flexible spending account, you have to earn $100 of salary to pay for $100 of medical expense deductions.

Caution. The drawback of a medical reimbursement plan is the "use it or lose it" feature. Any unused balance in your account at the end of the year belongs to your employer, not to you. So if at the beginning of the year you defer $1,000 into the medical reimbursement account but have only $500 of medical expenses during the year, you lose $500.

Under the other type of medical expense reimbursement account, the employer either directly reimburses employees for medical expenses up to a stated amount or makes payments directly to the provider of health care services. In either case, the payments are deductible by the employer and tax-free to the employee. The employer can fund the plan itself or buy insurance that will pay the benefits.

Insured medical plan. The other type of plan to consider is the insured medical plan. A health plan that is *not* considered an insured plan must meet nondiscrimination rules so it does not unduly favor highly paid employees, owners, and officers. But an insured medical plan does not have to meet nondiscrimination requirements. For example, an employer can set up an insured health plan by buying an insurance policy covering only one employee. It is quite common in large corporations for a few key executives to participate under the regular health plan and also have a separate insured health plan that provides additional benefits.

Employer-Paid Day Care

There are several ways for an employer to provide tax-free dependent care. A day care facility can be set up at or near the place of business. Or the employer can reimburse employees for the dependent care expenses they actually incur during the year.

A third option, when the employer offers a cafeteria benefit plan, is to allow employees to defer a certain amount of their salaries into flexible spending accounts to pay for dependent care. These are like the medical flexible spending accounts described in the previous section. The deferred money is not included in the employee's gross income. When an employee incurs dependent care assistance expenses, he or she is reimbursed from the account. These accounts have the same "use it or lose it" feature as medical expense reimbursement accounts.

Note that I have been using the term *dependent* care assistance. While child care is the most common type of dependent care assistance, this benefit also can be used for expenses incurred to pay for the care of a parent or other adult dependent.

Tax wise money strategy. Be sure you are taking full advantage of any dependent care assistance offered by your employer. If your employer does not provide dependent care assistance, encourage your employer to establish a flexible spending account or other form of dependent care assistance.

Up to $5,000 of dependent care assistance can be tax-free each year if the plan does not discriminate in favor of highly paid employees, officers, and shareholders. If you include employer-provided care from income, you cannot take the dependent and child-care tax credit for the same expenses. When a taxpayer is married, the amount of assistance excluded from income cannot exceed the earned income of the lower-earning spouse; for single taxpayers the tax-free amount cannot exclude earned income for the year.

Tax-Free Meals and Lodging

A surprising number of taxpayers, many of whom do not take advantage of this opportunity, qualify for tax-free employer-paid meals or lodging. If you qualify, meals and lodging for your spouse and dependents also are tax-free.

To be tax-free the meals and lodging must be provided on the business premises of the employer and for the convenience of the employer. For lodging to be tax-free, the employee also must be required to accept the lodging as a condition of employment. When the lodging qualifies as tax-free, auxiliary expenses such as utilities also are tax-free.

Tax-free meals and lodging often are provided to employees who operate a hotel, motel, restaurant, farm, or ranch. But other employees also can qualify. These rules are best explained by looking at one example when meals and lodging were tax-free and another when they were not.

Example. A married couple owned a hog farm and ran it as sole proprietors. They incorporated the farm, and the corporation hired them to manage it. As a condition of employment, the couple was required to live in the farmhouse and eat meals there because someone had to be around the farm at all times to look after the animals and handle emergencies. The corporation paid for the house and all related utilities. The IRS ruled that the meals and lodging were tax-free to the couple and deductible by the corporation (Private Letter Ruling 9134003).

Example. A married couple owned a ranch. They formed an S corporation to operate the ranch, named themselves officers of the corporation, and had the corporation provide their meals and lodging. But the couple, while officers of the corporation, did not have employment contracts with the corporation or receive salaries. Therefore the court ruled that they were not employees, and there was no business reason for them to be provided tax-free meals and lodging (*Dilts,* D.C. Wyo. 94-1 USTC 50, 162).

Supper money. "Supper money" is tax-free when it is paid occasionally to employees who perform extra work after regular working hours. Providing the supper money must be considered necessary to help the employee work the extra hours and must not be considered a form of additional compensation.

The IRS issued additional rules on supper money in 1994, because it felt that too many employers were giving supper money routinely as a way to provide tax-free compensation to employees. To be tax-free, the meals must be truly *de minimis* (small) in amount and be provided occasionally—not on a regular basis. And the meals must be provided to help the employee complete overtime work properly.

***De minimis* meals.** Periodic meals can be provided to employees if the benefit received by any employee is fairly small. The employer can pay for occasional working lunches or dinners, company picnics, and holiday parties without the employees being taxed on the value of these meals.

Tax wise money strategy. There are many occasions when meals or lodging can be furnished to employees tax-free. Sometimes these can be furnished on a continuing basis; at other times the employer can provide occasional tax-free meals. Employers and employees should look for ways to maximize these benefits.

Miscellaneous Benefits

In the late 1970s the IRS decided to tax virtually all fringe benefits. This created an uproar among taxpayers, and Congress responded by creating a group of fringe benefits that the IRS could not tax. These benefits are referred to as "statutory fringe benefits" and are in Section 132 of the tax code.

Statutory fringe benefits fall into these categories:

No-additional-cost services. An employer can provide employees with the services it sells to others in the normal course of business if the additional cost to the employer is no more than a nominal amount. For example, airlines can allow their employees to fly standby at no cost, and a telephone company can provide service to its employees.

Qualified employee discounts. Employees can receive tax-free discounts on goods and services sold to customers in the ordinary course of business. Discounts on services cannot exceed 20 percent, and discounts on goods cannot exceed the gross profit margin.

Working condition fringes. These are goods and services that are necessary for you to do your job. Common items in this category include business travel; subscriptions to business publications; and supplies, uniforms, and equipment. Here are some additional tax-free working condition fringe benefits:

• Employer-provided parking is tax-free up to a value of $155 per month. Any value of employer-provided parking above that amount must be included in gross income. Valuing parking spaces can be subjective.

Tax wise money strategy. Copy the IRS on this one. The IRS cut the taxable income on the parking it provides at its Washington, D.C., headquarters to its seventy-nine top executives by simply stating that each of them no longer had a specific reserved parking space. Instead, an area consisting of seventy-nine spaces is available only to these seventy-nine executives, and these employees can park in any of the seventy-nine spaces. The IRS said this little maneuver reduced the value of the spaces enough to save each of the employees over $700 per year in taxes.

• Commuting subsidies are tax-free up to $60 per month. The employer can provide transit passes for mass transportation facilities, vouchers for the passes, or cash reimbursements to employees when the passes are not readily available. The employer also can provide transportation on its own qualified commuter highway vehicles (vans).

• Chauffeur-driven cars are tax-free when necessary for security. There must have been an actual, realistic threat to an employee or to a prior employee in that person's position. In addition, the employee must be protected by the employer twenty-four hours a day for the secured transportation to be tax free, unless an independent security study says that twenty-four-hour security is not necessary; the employer must follow the recommendations of the study.

• Tax-free employer-paid education assistance is available when the education is job-related and either maintains or improves a current job skill, or is required to keep your present job. If the education qualifies you for a new job or position or helps you meet the minimum requirements for your job, then the additional education is not tax-free as a working condition fringe benefit.

De minimis **fringes.** These are benefits that are too small for the re-cordkeeping to be worthwhile. Examples include photocopying, occasional cocktail parties, typing or word processing services, subsidized eating facilities, group meals, local telephone calls, holiday and birthday gifts, and occasional tickets to theater or sporting events. Supper money for employees who occasionally work late, described earlier in this chapter, also is a *de minimis* fringe benefit. But if the value of these items grows to the point that the benefit can be considered a form of compensation, the items could be taxable.

On-premises athletic facilities. Tax-free facilities include gyms, pools, tennis courts, and golf courses. The facilities need not be available to the general public, and the premises can be either owned or leased by the employer.

Nondiscrimination required. No-additional-cost services, employee discounts, and subsidized eating facilities are tax-free only when there is no discrimination in favor of highly compensated employees, officers, and shareholders. The other statutory fringes are tax-free even if the employer discriminates among the employees to whom they are awarded.

Employee Achievement Awards

Safety and longevity awards can be tax-free to employees. An award must be made as part of a meaningful presentation and under circum-stances that do not indicate that it is disguised compensation.

If the award is issued under a written plan that does not discriminate in favor of highly compensated employees, the annual tax-free limit per employee is $1,600. Otherwise the limit is $400 per employee. Awards of cash, gift certificates, and equivalent items do not qualify for tax-free treatment.

Longevity awards can be awarded only after a minimum of five years of service, and there must be at least four years between longevity awards to an employee. Safety awards do not qualify if they are awarded to more than 10 percent of employees in a year, or if they are awarded to managers, administrators, clerical, or professional employees.

No-Interest Loans

No-interest loans can provide valuable benefits to employees, though Congress changed the rules to reduce the benefits.

When a business makes a loan to an employee, the loan is supposed to carry a minimum rate of interest determined by the IRS each month. If the minimum interest rate is not charged, the transaction will be treated as though the firm charged the employee the minimum rate of interest, then gave the employee additional compensation to cover the difference between the required minimum rate and the actual rate charged, which the employee in turn used to pay the imputed interest to the employer.

Example. ABC Corporation lends $50,000 to Max Profits, charging no interest. The minimum required interest rate is 8 percent. In the first year the imputed interest on the loan is $4,000. So the transaction is taxed as though Max received an additional $4,000 in compensation and paid that amount to ABC Corporation as interest. If Max is in the 36 percent tax bracket the loan costs him $1,620 in additional federal income taxes, or simple interest of 3.24 percent on the $50,000 loan.

Tax wise money strategy. If an employee has imputed interest income, he also can have imputed interest deductions. In the example, if the loan proceeds were used for investment purposes, Max could deduct the interest to the extent of his net investment income for the year. Or if the loan qualified as a mortgage loan (either to purchase or reconstruct a home or as a home equity loan) and is secured by Max's first or second home, the imputed interest could be deducted. When imputed interest is deductible, the interest-free loan rules result in a series of bookkeeping entries that offset each other. The employee gets a no-cost loan.

The imputed interest rules do not apply when the loan is $10,000 or less.

Expense Reimbursements

If you spend anything out of your pocket for employment-related expenses, you should consider asking your employer to set up an expense reimbursement plan.

All unreimbursed employment-related expenses you incur are deductible only as miscellaneous itemized expenses. That means you must itemize expenses to get any tax benefit, and can deduct only expenses that exceed 2 percent of adjusted gross income.

But expense reimbursements are tax-free when your employer sets up what is known as an "accountable plan." An accountable plan is one under which you have to turn in your receipts and give the employer the same details about the expenses that you would need to deduct them on your own return. The reimbursements avoid payroll taxes as well as income taxes.

Car reimbursements. If you drive your car for business, ask your employer to set up a mileage reimbursement plan. The employer would reimburse you at the IRS's standard mileage rate (29 cents per mile in 1994) for each business mile driven. Avoid getting a car allowance from the employer. That would be included in your income for the year and incur both income and payroll taxes.

Tax wise money strategy. Ask for a reimbursement plan instead of a pay raise. Suppose you earn $55,000 and pay $1,000 of unreimbursed employment-related expenses each year. You do not have enough miscellaneous itemized expenses to get a tax deduction. If your state has a 5 percent income tax, you have to earn $1,694.92 to have enough after-tax cash to pay for $1,000 of expenses. You would have much more after-tax cash if your employer reimbursed you for employment-related expenses instead of giving you a $1,000 raise.

The Offshore Advantage

Perhaps the best way to earn tax-free employment income and beat the 1993 tax hike is to work overseas. This allows you to earn up to $70,000 tax-free each year, and a tax-free housing allowance can be added to bring your tax-free income to more than $100,000 a year.

The exclusion is available only for earned income—that means either a salary or self-employment income. Interest, dividends, capital gains, royalties, annuities, and other types of investment or "unearned" income don't qualify. In addition, the exclusion does not apply if you work for the U.S. government or one of its agencies.

To qualify, you must establish a foreign tax home and pass either the foreign presence or foreign residence test. The foreign presence test says you must establish a foreign tax home and be out of the United States for at least 330 days during any twelve consecutive months. The rules for counting days are detailed and technical, so be sure to go over them with a tax adviser. The foreign residence test means you must have abandoned your previous residence and have an intention to stay outside of the United

States indefinitely. This is known as a "state of mind" test and is met by acts such as selling your United States home, changing your driver's license and car registration, and taking other official actions.

Benefits from Taxable Benefits

Not all fringe benefits are tax-free. But taxable fringe benefits usually are better than taking a taxable salary and paying for the expenses with after-tax money.

Example. Max Profits receives $5,000 of employer-paid financial counseling. This is a taxable benefit. Max includes $5,000 in his gross income, and in the 36 percent tax bracket that costs Max $1,800 in additional income taxes. But investment and tax advice are deductible as miscellaneous itemized expenses when the total miscellaneous expenses exceed 2 percent of adjusted gross income (AGI), even if Max does not pay directly for the services but has his employer pay the bill and add the amount to his gross income. If Max already has miscellaneous deductions exceeding 2 percent of AGI, he deduct, $5,000 and gets the services tax-free. To pay for this service himself, Max would have to earn $7,812.50 if he cannot deduct it and $5,000 (plus payroll taxes) if the entire expense is deductible. At worst, Max pays $1,800 for $5,000 of services; at best, he gets the services free. That is why taxable benefits can be better than a salary increase.

Payroll tax alert. Many taxable fringe benefits are subject to payroll taxes, even if deductions wipe out the income taxes. So Max also would pay 1.45 percent for the Medicare/Medicaid tax and, if his wages are not above the Social Security maximum, another 6.2 percent for Social Security taxes.

Tax wise money strategy. Financial counseling is one of the most popular taxable benefits. Additional taxable benefits include the use of vacation homes or condos, personal automobiles, club memberships, home security systems, executive dining rooms, home computers, cellular telephones, and home fax machines. By having the employer pay for these items and add the value to your gross income, you get the benefit of these items for a fraction of the real cost. Virtually any expense you have can become a taxable fringe benefit.

Tax-Exempt Fringe Benefits Checklist

This checklist of widely available tax-free employee fringe benefits is not exhaustive, because there are many items that can be provided tax-free but have not received an IRS ruling. A number of these benefits are tax-free only under certain limits, conditions, and qualifications. For example, *de minimis* fringe benefits must be infrequent or low in cost to be tax-free. So check with a tax adviser before setting up a specific benefit plan.

Athletic facilities on the employer premises
Accident and health insurance premiums and benefits
Cafeteria fringe benefit plans
Car provided by employer and used for business
Child and dependent care benefits
Death benefits, employer-paid, up to $5,000
Educational assistance, employer-provided
Foreign earned income, up to $70,000 plus housing allowance
Incentive stock options
Interest-free loans, *de minimis* amounts
Life insurance, group term policy up to $50,000 coverage
Lodging required as a condition of employer, furnished for employer's convenience on the premises
Meals furnished on the employer's premises for the employer's convenience
Medical care reimbursement plans
Mileage allowance for business use of personal car
Pension plan contributions
Sickness and injury benefits
Supper money for overtime work
***De minimis* fringe benefits**
- Birthday gifts, other than cash with low market value
- Light refreshments (coffee, soda, doughnuts)
- Eating facility, employer-operated
- Gifts for illness, family emergency, outstanding performance (flowers, books, fruit, etc.)
- Group term life insurance on spouse or child
- Local telephone calls
- Photocopy machine use
- Meal money
- Occasional parties, picnics, group meals with employees and guests
- Theater and sporting event tickets
- Typing of personal letters

No-additional-cost services
Qualified employee discounts on employer's goods and services
Qualified moving expense reimbursements
Qualified transportation fringes
- Parking not to exceed $155 per month
- Transit passes not exceeding $60 per month
- Commuting in a computer highway vehicle

Working condition fringes
- Air transportation, for business use only
- Automobile demos
- Chauffeur services for business use, not commuting
- Flexible spending accounts
- Outplacement services
- Transportation for security reasons, including chauffeur/bodyguard

Chapter 3

Maximizing Tax-Free Investment Income: Avoiding Traps That Cost You Money

Higher tax rates can make tax-exempt bonds more attractive than taxable alternatives. After the 1993 tax hike, taxpayers in at least twelve states face combined state and federal maximum tax rates of more than 41 percent.

Unfortunately, all tax-exempt opportunities are *not* the same. Many people are investing in tax-exempt products with lower after-tax returns than taxable investments or that take high risks.

This chapter shows you how to select the tax-exempt investment opportunity that maximizes the bottom line—after all taxes and expenses are considered—without increasing risk.

Is Tax-Exempt Investing for You?

Interest paid on the debt issued by state and local governments generally is exempt from federal income tax. Most states exempt from their income taxes all interest income from bonds issued by the state or its localities. A few states exempt interest paid on any state or local government bonds.

A price you pay for earning tax-free interest is that the yield usually is less than you could earn from comparable taxable debt. Historically, tax-exempt bonds pay yields from 65 percent to 95 percent of Treasury debt. You need to compare the yield on tax-exempt debt to the after-tax yield from taxable debt to see if tax-exempt investing is for you.

Tax wise money strategy. To compare a tax-exempt yield with the after-tax yield on a taxable investment, subtract your marginal tax rate from 1. If your marginal tax rate is 28 percent, the subtraction gives you 0.72. That means for each dollar of taxable interest, you keep 72 cents. Multiply the yield you can earn on a taxable investment by 0.72, and that gives you the after-tax yield (also known as the tax-exempt equivalent yield). If the tax-exempt yield is higher than the after-tax yield, tax-exempt investing could be for you.

An alternative is to divide 0.72 into the tax-free yield you expect to receive. The result is the "taxable equivalent yield." That is the amount a taxable investment has to yield before taxes to give you the same after-tax yield as the tax-exempt investment.

Example. You are in the 28 percent marginal federal income tax bracket. You can choose between a taxable bond yielding 5.75 percent, and a tax-free bond yielding 4.3 percent. When you subtract 0.28 from 1, you get 0.72. Multiplying that by the taxable yield of 5.75 percent gives you 4.14 percent. That is what the taxable investment would yield after taxes. Since the tax-free investment yields 4.3 percent, the tax-free investment is the better deal, looking strictly at the yields.

Using the alternative approach, you could divide the tax-exempt yield of 4.3 percent by 0.72 and get 5.97 percent. That is how much the taxable investment would have to yield to give you the same after-tax return as the tax-free investment.

Tax wise money strategy. When comparing yields, be sure the investments are similar. Some promotions compare long-term tax-free bond yields to those of money market funds or certificates of deposit. Long-term bonds have higher yields than money market funds and CDs because the bonds are more volatile.

As a general rule, the longer the maturity of the bonds, the more attractive tax-exempts are. With short-term debt, particularly money market funds, there is a smaller yield difference between taxable and tax-exempt yields. So exempt interest income often is not worthwhile with shorter maturities, even to those in the highest tax brackets.

Lessons for Yield Chasers

Examining yields is only the beginning of your investment search. Yield chasers often end up either losing money or accumulating less money than they could have earned from lower-yielding or taxable alternatives. Here are other factors to consider before putting money into a tax-exempt (or any other) investment.

Safety

Tax-exempt bonds are not risk-free. Some states and localities have defaulted on bonds.

In addition, different bonds issued by the same state or locality have different degrees of safety. A "general revenue bond" is backed by the general taxing and spending power of a government. It is considered the safest debt a government issues. No state has defaulted on in its general obligation bonds since the Civil War.

But many agencies, authorities, and other subdivisions of a state issue debt that often is backed only by the earnings or revenue of a particular project or agency. If the project, such as a toll road or industrial park, does not generate enough revenue, the bonds or interest might not be paid in full on time.

The safest tax-exempt bonds usually are either general obligation bonds (backed by the general taxing power) or revenue bonds that finance essential government operations (such as roads and bridges). The riskiest bonds are revenue bonds that finance hospitals and airports.

Insured bonds. Exempt bonds can be insured by private firms. The insurance is as good as the financial strength of the insurers.

Your yield is reduced to pay for the insurance, usually by 0.25 percent. The insurers obviously are going to insure only bonds that are fairly secure. Bonds with significant risk are not going to get insurance. If you buy bonds backed by hospitals, airports, or similar projects, you probably want them insured. But with general obligation bonds, you probably are paying for security you are not likely to need with insured bonds. You might be better off getting uninsured revenue bonds from fiscally sound governments and pocketing the extra yield.

Call Risk

Many tax-exempt bonds give the issuer the right to repay the bonds without a penalty. Usually the bonds can be prepaid or "called" five years after the bonds were issued. Some bonds can be called at any time after that. Other bonds must be called within certain time frames.

When a tax-exempt bond is called, you get your principal back and must reinvest it if you still want to earn income. Bonds usually are called when interest rates have fallen, so you will have to accept a lower yield than the one you just lost.

If you buy a ten-year bond that can be called after five years, you can count on that yield for five years only. After that, either the bond will be called or market interest rates will be at least as high as the yield on your bond.

Liquidity

There is no central exchange or ready market for exempt bonds, as there is with stocks and Treasury bonds. Most state and local bond issues are too small for brokers to follow regularly or try to make a market.

Table 1
Tax-Exempt-Yield Calculator: Is Tax-Exempt Investing for You?

If your Taxable Yield is (in percent):

And Your Tax Rate Is:	3	3.5	4	4.5	5	5.5	6	6.5	7	7.5	8	8.5	9
	Your Tax-Exempt Equivalent Is (in percent):												
15%	2.55	2.975	3.4	3.825	4.25	4.675	5.1	5.525	5.95	6.375	6.8	7.225	7.65
28%	2.16	2.52	2.88	3.24	3.6	3.96	4.32	4.68	5.04	5.4	5.76	6.12	6.48
31%	2.07	2.415	2.76	3.105	3.45	2.795	4.14	4.485	4.83	5.175	5.52	5.865	6.21
36%	1.92	2.24	2.56	2.88	3.2	3.52	3.84	4.16	4.48	4.8	5.12	5.44	5.76
39.6%	1.812	2.114	2.416	2.718	3.02	3.322	3.624	3.926	4.228	4.53	4.832	5.134	5.436

If Your Tax-Exempt Yield Is (in percent):

And Your Tax Rate Is:	3	3.5	4	4.5	5	5.5	6	6.5	7	7.5	8	8.5	9
	Your Taxable Equivalent Yield Is (in percent):												
15%	3.53	4.12	4.71	5.29	5.88	6.47	7.06	7.65	8.24	8.82	9.41	10.00	10.59
28%	4.17	4.86	5.56	6.25	6.94	7.64	8.33	9.03	9.72	10.42	11.11	11.81	12.50
31%	4.35	5.07	5.80	6.52	7.25	7.97	8.70	9.42	10.14	10.87	11.59	12.32	13.04
36%	4.69	5.47	6.25	7.03	7.81	8.59	9.38	10.16	10.94	11.72	12.50	13.28	14.06
39.6%	4.97	5.79	6.62	7.45	8.28	9.11	9.93	10.76	11.59	12.42	13.25	14.07	14.90

When you want to sell you have to look hard for a brokerage firm that will make an offer, which often is rather low. In other words, if you need to sell a tax-exempt bond, you could easily end up giving it to a broker at a big discount.

The lack of an organized market also is a problem when you want to *buy* tax-free bonds. If you buy from a broker, you probably will be paying a fairly sizable markup over what the broker paid for the bond and will not have many sellers to choose from.

Mutual fund solution. Investing through mutual funds partially solves the liquidity problem. The fund will redeem shares each day as investors request. But there are a couple of potential problems. Mutual funds tend to put a portion of their portfolios in bonds that will not be easy to sell, because those bonds pay higher yields than more liquid bonds. When interest rates rise, bond values fall, and if a number of investors decide to cash out of tax-exempt bond funds at once, there are big problems. The funds will have to sell the most liquid, highest-quality bonds first to pay the investors who want redemptions, and prices of those bonds will crash. There will not be any buyers for other issues.

A minipanic of this sort happened in early 1987 when interest rates rose. Another happened in early 1994 when interest rates rose sharply. Some bond funds reported that they had trouble even getting reliable price quotes for many of their bonds. Without reliable price quotes, it is not easy for mutual funds to determine the net asset value of shares each day and to know how much to pay investors who want shares redeemed. The bond funds sold their highest-quality bonds to meet redemptions, and the reported values of the remaining bonds were educated guesses. In truth, the funds could not have sold many of these bonds at any price if they needed to.

An investor who buys individual bonds and plan to hold them until maturity does not have to worry about liquidity. But other tax-exempt bond investors need to accept that periodically there will be serious liquidity problems in the tax-exempt bond market and that there is not much protection.

Maturity

Most bond investors focus on yield. But the value of your bonds or bond funds is not fixed. As interest rates rise and fall, the value of your principal does the opposite.

Long-term bonds (those with maturity dates more than ten years in the future) are the most volatile. When interest rates fall 1 percent, a long-term bond's value could rise 10 percent or more. But the value can fall by 10 percent or more when interest rates rise, because newer bonds offer higher yields. Long-term bonds generally offer higher yields than shorter-term bonds to make up for this risk.

When you plan to hold a bond to maturity, the principal fluctuations probably don't matter to you. But if you invest in a mutual fund or plan to sell a bond before it matures, then you need to pay attention to maturity dates.

If interest rates are low or have declined substantially, you want to avoid long-term bonds.

Double-Tax-Free Bonds

When a state income tax exempts interest earned on debt issued by the state, bonds issued within the state are known as double-tax-free for its residents. They avoid both federal and state income taxes on the interest. When a locality also has an income tax, you can get triple-tax-free bonds. For example, New York City residents get triple-tax-free income from New York City debt. The interest earned on that debt is exempt from federal, state, and city income taxes. Except in a few states, interest earned on bonds of another state will be exempt from federal income taxes but taxed by your state. When a mutual fund buys only the bonds issued in one state, it is known as a single-state or double-tax-free bond fund.

But buying a double-tax-free bond or fund is not always better than buying single-tax-free bonds or funds. The single-tax-free bonds might pay a higher after-tax yield than the double-tax-frees.

Tax wise money strategy. To determine if you should buy a single- or a double-tax-exempt bond or fund, use the same calculation you used to determine if you should buy a taxable or tax-exempt bond, but add your state income tax rate.

Example. If you are in the 28 percent federal tax bracket and 5 percent state tax bracket, your combined tax rate is 33 percent. You subtract .33 from 1 and get 0.67. If you can earn 5.75 percent on a taxable investment, that is an after-tax yield of 3.85 percent. A single state fund has to earn a higher yield than that for you to consider investing in it.

If a double-tax-free fund yields 4.3 percent, divide that by 0.67. A taxable fund must yield 6.42 or higher than that to beat the double-tax-free fund.

Suppose you can get a 4.5 percent yield from a national tax-exempt bond fund and have a 5 percent state tax rate. To determine the after-tax yield, multiply 0.95 by 4.5 percent. Your after-tax yield from the national tax-free fund is 4.28 percent. So you come out a little bit ahead in the double-tax-exempt fund in this example.

Here is a summary of the calculations:

	Pretax Yield	After-Tax Yield
National exempt	4.5%	4.28%
Double exempt	4.3%	4.3%
Taxable investment	5.75%	3.85%

An important disadvantage of single-state funds is that they tend to hold mostly long-term bonds. These can lose value if interest rates rise, and also are likely to be called if interest rates fall.

AMT alert. Interest earned on "private activity" or "nongovernmental function" state and local bonds is taxed under the alternative minimum tax. The bonds, sometimes called AMT bonds, pay for activities that are not considered the core functions of government. The interest on the bonds still are tax-free under the regular income tax.

Tax wise money strategy. If you might be subject to the AMT and invest in a tax-exempt mutual fund, contact the fund to determine how much of its portfolio is invested in AMT bonds.

Tax wise money strategy. AMT bonds are a big advantage if you are *not* subject to the AMT. The bonds pay a higher yield than non-AMT bonds because they might be subject to tax. So you can get a higher tax-free yield by investing in AMT bonds. But the AMT bonds tend to be riskier because they do fund nonessential government functions and usually are not fully backed or guaranteed by a government.

Tax-Sheltered Treasury Debt

Interest earned on U.S government debt is taxed under federal income tax. But the U.S. Supreme Court has ruled that states cannot tax interest on federal government debt. Most states accept that this rule applies to interest that mutual funds earn on federal Treasury debt and distribute to their shareholders.

Tax wise money strategy. If your state has an income tax, interest income on Treasury debt is tax-free on your state return. This pushes up the after-tax return and could make Treasury debt a better after-tax investment than tax-exempt bonds, especially if you live in a state with high income-tax rates.

You decide when federal debt is a good deal by using the same calculation we used in the other situations.

Example. Your state imposes a 9 percent income-tax rate, and your federal tax rate is 31 percent. You could earn 5 percent on a U.S. Treasury bond that is exempt from state taxes or 3.5 percent on a national tax-exempt bond fund that is not exempt from state taxes. The after-tax yield on the Treasury bond is 3.45 percent. You get a higher after-tax return from the Treasury bond.

Best Ways to Invest

There are several ways to invest in tax-exempt bonds: individual bonds, unit investment trusts, and mutual funds. Here is how to decide which is best for you.

Individual Bonds

You can buy U.S. government bonds directly from the Treasury and save the commissions and markups of brokers. But you can't do that with most state bonds. An individual who wants to buy state and local bonds usually must buy from a broker.

All studies show that you pay handsomely for buying individual bonds through a broker. There is a markup on the bonds depending on how many of the bonds the broker has and how many people want to buy the bonds. Often the statement you receive after a transaction does not reveal the markup.

You can call among brokers and get very different quotes for the same or similar bonds. This is a market where the little guy does not get a good deal. You will not get a good price at all unless you plan to invest at least $25,000 per bond issue. If you are looking to buy a diversified portfolio of issues and maturities, you will need quite a bit of money to get a portfolio at good prices.

Some tax-exempt-bond issuers are trying to reduce these problems by experimenting with smaller bonds of $5,000 or so (called baby bonds) that can be purchased directly from the issuer.

Selling individual bonds is no better. You are at the mercy of whatever the brokers want to offer—when you can find one who will bid on your bonds. Therefore you should not buy individual bonds unless you are fairly certain to hold them until maturity.

Several scandals prompted investigations into these problems. The September 6, 1993, issue of *Business Week* summarized the investigations and concluded that because of the markups, hidden commissions, small number of market makers, and political payoffs, individual investors are likely to get burned by purchasing individual exempt bonds.

The Securities and Exchange Commission (SEC) also looked into the problems and changed some of the rules for brokers. But the SEC cannot change the fact that this market is not favorable to the individual investor, and huge markups are likely to continue.

Another disadvantage of individual bonds is that they can be recalled by the issuer.

Tax wise money strategy. If, after considering all these potential disadvantages, you still want to invest in individual exempt bonds, be sure to assemble a portfolio that is diversified among both issuers and maturities. You'll need at least $100,000. It is a good idea to invest at least 25 percent of your exempt bond portfolio outside your state. In that way, if your state's economy fares poorly, you are diversified by being invested in another state that might not suffer from economic problems. Otherwise, at least buy from different issuers within the state.

The bond ladder. You should stagger the maturities of the bonds in a bond ladder. Let's say you can afford to buy ten different bonds. Buy one bond that matures in one year; one that matures in two years, etc. When the original one-year bond matures, you reinvest the proceeds in a ten-year bond. In that way you always have a complete ladder of bonds.

The advantage of the bond ladder is that it keeps you from being hurt too much by calls, rising interest rates, or being locked into low-yielding investments.

Mutual Funds and Unit Trusts

Most investors should stick with mutual funds or unit investment trusts (UITs). There are important differences between the two vehicles, and you need to know them to find which vehicle is better for you.

A tax-exempt open-end mutual fund is just like any other mutual fund. It takes money from shareholders, buys tax-exempt debt, redeems shares when investors request, and passes interest and gains through to shareholders. A fund can be load or no-load. A load fund subtracts a commission from your initial investment; a no-load fund does not. The fund manager will trade the portfolio within the fund's investment objectives.

A UIT buys and holds a fixed set of bonds. Investors usually but not always are told in advance which issues will be purchased. Some UITs are permitted to sell when there is a concern about default. Otherwise the manager generally collects interest payments and delivers them to investors along with annual reports. When the bonds mature, the trust collects the principal and distributes it to investors.

With a UIT there usually is an up-front commission of 4 percent or so. An annual fee of 0.5 percent is charged to collect the interest and pass it on to investors.

Unlike a mutual fund, a UIT is very difficult to sell. The brokerage firm that sold the UIT might offer to buy back the units, but not at a very attractive price. Otherwise, the investor must hope that his or her broker can find a buyer willing to take the shares.

When a UIT is put together by a brokerage firm, it is possible that some bad bonds the firm cannot otherwise sell will be dumped in with some good bonds. Some analysts say this is a common practice.

Tax wise money strategy. If you like the concept of a UIT, perhaps the best way to invest is to buy used units from an investor who wants to bail out. You can get an attractive price, and the UIT already will have a performance history. These opportunities generally can be located through the brokerage firms that sold the UITs originally. But it is difficult to determine the true yield of a used UIT. You probably will need the advice of a financial adviser experienced in this area.

The differences between UITs and mutual funds are summarized in the following table.

Table 2
Mutual Funds vs. Unit Investment Trusts

Mutual Funds	Unit Investment Trusts
Load or no-load	Commission on sale
Annual expenses	Annual expenses
Managed portfolio	Usually unmanaged portfolio
Redeemable shares	Illiquid shares
Can avoid calls on bonds	Bonds subject to calls
Might mismanage interest rate changes	Doesn't manage interest rate changes

Tax wise money strategy: For most investors, a no-load mutual fund with low expenses is the best way to buy tax-exempts. It is difficult for a bond mutual fund to get a substantially higher yield than another fund, because the market determines yields. Loads and fees are the biggest determinants of whether you get a superior return or a mediocre one. In fact, you often are better off in a taxable investment than in an exempt mutual fund that has a load or high annual expenses.

Closed-End Bond Funds

Closed-end bond funds are mutual funds that trade on the stock exchanges like regular stocks.

Closed-end funds usually sell at either a premium to or discount from their asset values. For example, suppose a closed-end mutual fund holds bonds worth $10 million. If it trades at a 10 percent discount from its net asset value, then the fund's shares are trading at a total value of only $9 million. If the net asset value behind each share is $100, then you can buy a share for $90 and basically get $10 worth of bonds free with each share.

This is where things get interesting. Suppose a closed-end fund was invested to yield 8 percent tax-free. But suppose also that the shares trade at a discount of 15 percent. Then if you buy shares at the discounted value, your yield jumps to 9.41 percent tax-free. Over time the market should catch on and the share price should rise so that the discount on the shares is reduced. You then could get a double benefit by selling at a capital gain.

Tax wise money strategy. There are times when tax-exempt bond closed-end funds sell at substantial discounts from their net asset values and you can implement the strategy described above. But sometimes a closed-end fund is selling at a substantial discount because it is holding risky or bad investments or there is something wrong with management. Make sure the discount is due to market conditions and not a problem with that fund.

Not Totally Tax-Free

Your tax-exempt bond investment might be taxed in several different ways.

When interest rates fall, the value of a bond rises. If you sell the bond, you will have a capital gain. After the 1993 tax changes, you might have ordinary income instead of capital gains on the sale of bonds. The new rules say that if you buy an individual bond for less than its face amount, then on a subsequent sale the difference between the purchase price and the face amount is ordinary income. Any additional gain is capital gain.

Mutual fund investors have capital gains if they sell the fund shares for more than they cost. But a mutual fund investor also could have taxable capital gains when no shares are sold. The mutual fund buys and sells a number of bonds during the year, and any net capital gain is distributed and taxed to the shareholders.

Your exempt bonds also are potentially subject to estate taxes. Bonds are property just like any other, so the value is included in your estate. You must use regular estate planning strategies if you want the value of the bonds to avoid estate taxes.

Chapter 4

The "Family Device": Using the Tax Code to Maximize Family Wealth

Different members of your family are likely to have different marginal tax rates. You can use this situation to increase after-tax wealth by shifting income and deductions to where the tax burdens will be the lowest and tax benefits the highest. The "family device" is the simple principle that, when possible, income and gains should be shifted to family members in lower tax brackets.

Example. Max and Rosie Profits are in the 45 percent federal and state tax bracket and earn about $20,000 of interest and dividends. The Profits must pay about $9,000 of taxes on their investment income, leaving them with only $11,000 to reinvest. Max and Rosie do not need this investment income to meet their current living expenses and plan to use a large part of the portfolio to pay for the college expenses of their two children. To reduce the tax burden, Max and Rosie give some of the portfolio to their children, each of whom is in the 15 percent tax bracket. The result is that eighty-five percent of each investment dollar earned by the children is reinvested.

Tax wise money strategy. Family income shifting is highly recommended for parents trying to save for college tuition, because the lower tax rates boost the tuition fund faster. Grandparents also can use income shifting with both their adult children and their grandchildren.

Avoiding the "Kiddie Tax"

Congress doesn't like the family device. So in 1986 it created the "kiddie tax."

The kiddie tax has three basic provisions:

• No personal exemption can be claimed by someone who can be claimed as a dependent on the tax return of another person. It doesn't matter if the other person chooses not to claim the exemption; if the person qualifies to claim the exemption, the dependent does not get a personal exemption.

• A taxpayer who is the dependent of another (usually a child) gets only a $500 (indexed for inflation) standard deduction to offset investment income. If the child has earned income, he or she can take the regular standard deduction to the extent of earned income. So the first $500 of investment income of a child under age fourteen is tax-free.

• The taxable "unearned" (investment) income of a child under age fourteen that exceeds $500 per year (indexed for inflation) is taxed at the top rate of the parents. The first $500 of taxable investment income is taxed at the child's rate, usually 15 percent. This tax is computed on Form 8615, which must be included with the child's tax return.

The third part of the kiddie tax applies only to children under fourteen. Once a child turns fourteen, all investment income that he or she earns is taxed at the child's tax rate.

That, in a nutshell, is the kiddie tax. Here's how to beat it.

The Double Exemption

Inflation indexing brought both the kiddie tax exemption and the standard deduction mentioned above to $600 each in 1994. That means that a child under age fourteen can earn $600 of investment income tax-free, and have another $600 taxed at the child's tax rate. Only after $1,200 of investment income is earned by the child is the income taxed at the parents' top tax rate.

Example. Minnie Profits is age ten and was given some investment assets by her parents that produced $1,700 of interest and dividend income last year. This is all of Minnie's income. The first $600 is offset by the standard deduction and not taxed. The second $600 is taxed at the 15 percent rate. The remaining $500 is taxed at her parents' 39.6 rate. Minnie's tax for the year is $288, or about 17 percent of her income. If her parents still owned the investments, they would have paid $594 in taxes, so the Profits saved $221 using the family device.

Parents' Election

Parents who want to avoid the cost and trouble of filing a tax return for their children can elect to include the child's investment income on their own returns and pay the kiddie tax themselves. A parent is eligible for this election when the child's gross income consists solely of interest, dividends, and Alaska Permanent Fund dividends, and is more than $500 but less than $5,000.

To claim the election the parent must file Form 8814 for each child when the election is made, so the trouble of filing the return for the child is reduced only slightly.

In addition, the $500 base amount for the parents' election is not indexed for inflation. So for 1994, the parents who make this election pay their maximum tax rate after the first $1,000 of the child's income, while the child would pay the top rate only after $1,200 of investment income. Therefore, taking this election increases income taxes.

Family Wealth-Building Strategies

There are many tax wise money strategies that split income among family members while avoiding the effects of the kiddie tax. Here are the best methods available.

Squeezing Under the Kiddie Tax Floor

When a child is under age fourteen, the first $1,200 of investment income avoids the kiddie tax. If the money is earning 8 percent, that means that an investment portfolio of up to $15,000 avoids the kiddie tax. At a 6 percent return, a portfolio of up to $20,000 avoids the kiddie tax.

Tax wise money strategy. Start shifting income to your children without worrying about the kiddie tax. You can start worrying about the kiddie tax when the account balance and income start hitting the kiddie tax trigger levels.

Kiddie Tax Investing

When your children's investment portfolios are ready to start generating investment income above the safe ceiling amount of $1,200, a few simple changes in the investment allocation of the portfolio are enough to avoid the kiddie tax.

Tax wise money strategy. When the kiddie tax is a danger, shift some of the portfolio into assets that will not produce current income. Ideal investments are those that defer income or that earn capital gains that compound over time. Appropriate investments include:

- U.S. savings bonds;
- tax-exempt bonds;
- stocks that don't pay dividends;
- raw land

- U.S. Treasury bills;
- some certificates of deposit;
- mutual funds with low annual distributions;
- annuities.

The portfolio needs to be invested in this way only until the child turns fourteen.

Lowering Capital Gains Taxes
The maximum tax rate on long-term capital gains is 28 percent. That is substantially lower than the 39.6 percent rate on ordinary income, but it still is too high for many investors.

Tax wise money strategy. When you have a child age fourteen or older, one way to slash capital gains taxes is to give the appreciated property to the child. Then have your child sell the property. Be sure that you give no more property than qualifies for the annual gift tax exclusion described later in this chapter.

Example. You hold mutual fund shares worth $20,000, and your basis in the shares is $12,000. Your capital gain is $8,000, with a potential tax of $2,240. If you give the shares to your fifteen-year-old who sells them immediately, the capital gains tax rate at the child's rate of 15 percent is only $1,200. You save almost $1,000, or 5 percent of the total value, by having your child sell the shares.

Hiring Your Children
Business owners can hire their children and pay them salaries. This strategy yields several tax benefits:

- The salary paid the children is earned income, not investment income. So the kiddie tax does not apply no matter how young the children are and how much money they earn.
- The salary is deductible by the business when the children do real work and the salary is reasonable considering the work done and the skills of the children. So if you are a sole proprietor, the salary is deducted from your self-employment income (reducing your income taxes and the self-employment tax) and taxed at the child's rate.
- If the business is unincorporated and the child is under age eighteen, you do not have to pay or withhold Social Security taxes on the salary.

Tax wise money strategy. Putting a child on the payroll allows the child to earn up to the standard deduction amount tax-free each year ($3,800 in 1994). The child can increase tax-free income to $5,800 by making a deductible $2,000 IRA contribution.

Put Your Children on the Board

Often a child is away from home at college, or working in the business requires special skills that the child does not have. In these cases, you can split income with the child by putting him or her on the board of directors. Once again, the child has earned income that is deductible by the business. You must be sure that the child is old enough and has sufficient background to justify the director's compensation.

Leasing Assets to the Business

Most businesses need some kind of equipment, including an office building. A tax-advantaged way to provide this equipment is to have your children buy the equipment and lease it to the business. The lease payments will be deductible by the business. In addition, the children will be able to depreciate the equipment against the rental income, and the rest will be taxed at the children's tax rate.

You probably don't want to have the children own the equipment directly. There are other options:

• A trust can own the equipment. The trustee can manage the equipment, collect the rent, and decide how much income to distribute to the children.

• An S corporation owned by the children can own the equipment. The income and expenses of the corporation pass through to the children, and the children can own only nonvoting stock.

• A partnership consisting of the children owns the equipment. The partnership is more flexible than the S corporation.

Tax wise money strategy. Instead of having the children buy new equipment, you can give them existing equipment. The gift-leaseback is especially valuable when the equipment already was fully depreciated but still has many years of use left. The children in their tax brackets don't need the high depreciation of brand-new equipment, while the business replaces the exhausted depreciation deduction with lease deductions.

Caution. In the leasing transactions, the income usually is considered investment income to the children, so the kiddie tax applies.

Best result. When you or the business owns real estate, give the land to the children. Keep the building, so you or the business will get the depreciation deductions. By leasing the land from the children you get to deduct lease payments on the land, which is not depreciable.

Leaseback-Loan Combination

Suppose your business leases property from your children as described. You then can borrow back from the children the lease income they receive. If the loan proceeds are used in your business, you should be able to deduct the interest payments you make to the children.

Sharing Business Income

When your business produces more income than your current needs, consider sharing ownership of the business with other family members. Dividends and distributions can be spread among the family and taxed at different rates. The two most common ways to share ownership to split income are the S corporation and the family partnership.

The S corporation has more technical requirements than the partnership; it is easy to run afoul of the requirements and lose S corporation status. A partnership is more flexible, but to split business income using a partnership, the business income must not be earned largely by the efforts of the parent. Capital must be a material income-producing factor in the business.

Audit alert. Some of these income-splitting strategies are straightforward and can be implemented without many problems. But several of the strategies, especially those involving businesses, are complicated and have many qualifications. You should not attempt these without the help of an experienced tax professional. If the paperwork is not done according to IRS standards, you lose the benefit of income shifting and will have to pay interest and penalties as well.

College aid alert. Anyone seeking financial aid for college (grants, loans, student employment) must complete a standard financial aid form and is subject to the Expected Family Contribution (EFC) rules.

Under EFC, a family's income, assets, and the number of children in college determine how much of a financial contribution the family is expected to make to the college expenses. Under EFC, a child is expected to use 35 percent of any assets in the child's name. By comparison, parents earning $20,000 are expected to contribute only 5.6 percent of their assets and income for college. So shifting assets and income to a child's name might save you income taxes now but cost you financial aid in the future. You might avoid this problem by shifting the assets back from the child to the parent before it is time to apply for aid. But this could be difficult if the assets are held in an UGMA account, 2503(c) trust, or irrevocable trust. There also might be a gift tax on the transfer if the value of the assets exceeds $10,000 per parent. Those most likely to be hurt by this situation are families with incomes between $50,000 and $150,000.

How to Give Money Away Profitably

To make the family device work, you obviously have to give money and property away to others, usually your children. You want to avoid gift taxes, which can be higher than income taxes, while ensuring that the property will not be wasted or squandered.

To avoid gift taxes, you must qualify for the annual gift-tax exclusion by giving each donee no more than $10,000 each year ($20,000 if you are married and give jointly with your spouse). But to qualify for the gift-tax exclusion, the gift must be a "present interest." That means that if it comes with too many strings attached or if you might be able to get the gift back, it is not a gift of a present interest and does not qualify for the exclusion. More details on gift taxes are in Chapter 20, on estate planning.

Fortunately, the tax code provides several ways of qualifying for the gift-tax exclusion without giving children complete control of the property.

UGMA Account

Gifts to an account established under the Uniform Gift to Minors Act (UGMA) qualify for the exclusion. You simply deposit money for your child in an account at a financial institution designed as an UGMA account and name yourself or some other adult custodian of the account.

The income is taxed to the child, but the custodian controls investments and withdrawals. The tax code states that putting money in a UGMA qualifies for the gift-tax exclusion.

The downside of the UGMA is that the money becomes the sole property of the child when the child reaches the age of majority—either eighteen or twenty-one, depending on the state. This conversion is automatic, and there is nothing you legally can do to prevent it or to control the money after the child comes of age. That means the child can take the money and go on a cruise or buy a car instead of paying for college. Another disadvantage of the UGMA is that when the custodian also is the person who made the gift to the UGMA, the UGMA will be included in that person's estate if he or she should die before the child reaches age of majority.

Section 2503(c) Trust

This is a special trust in the tax law. The gift to the trust qualifies for the annual gift-tax exclusion if under the terms of the trust the property and income may be expended for the benefit of a minor before age twenty-one, and any remaining trust property becomes the child's upon reaching age twenty-one. This trust is helpful in states where the child would get the property at age eighteen under a UGMA, and it also avoids having the property included in your estate if you die before the child reaches age twenty-one.

Irrevocable Trusts

For large gifts, you probably want to go through the expense and trouble of creating an irrevocable trust.

An irrevocable trust can have a spendthrift clause so that trust assets cannot be attached by the child's creditors or pledged for debts. You can give the trustee the discretion to decide when income and principal will be distributed, or you can give firm rules for the distribution of property.

Another advantage of the trust is that you can obtain professional management of the trust assets if the trust is large enough. An irrevocable trust also is excluded from your estate when the trust is set up properly.

To qualify for the annual gift-tax exclusion, annual gifts to the trust must come with at least one of two rights. One right gives the trust beneficiary (the child) the continuing right to compel immediate distribution of trust assets at any time. The other right, which is used most often, allows the beneficiary the right during a limited period after a gift is made to the trust, usually thirty days, to compel immediate distribution of the gift. If the right is not exercised within the time period, the beneficiary no longer can compel the distribution of that gift or its future income. This second right is known as a *Crummey* provision, after the court case that established it.

Tax wise money strategy. An irrevocable trust potentially has another tax advantage. If income is not distributed from the trust, it normally is taxed at the trust's tax rate. This gives you a third taxpayer among which to split income and reduce overall taxes: you, the trust, and the child. When the trustee has discretion over distributions from the trust and considers taxes as one factor when planning distributions, annual income taxes can be minimized.

Tax wise money strategy. The UGMA account or Section 2503(c) trust will meet the needs of most parents. The amount of money involved often is not enough to justify the cost of setting up and maintaining an irrevocable trust. If the child seems too irresponsible to make good use of the account, it is not too difficult for you to see that the money is spent on appropriate items before the child gets control. Parents who will give a lot to their children or who have especially unpredictable children will want to set up irrevocable trusts. Most irrevocable trusts are set up to last longer than the child's college years.

Caution. When trust income is used to pay for items that are the legal support obligations of the parent, the income used to pay for those items is taxable to the parent. In some states, college education is considered a legal support obligation, but in most states it is not.

Chapter 5

Tax Wise Mutual Fund Investing
for the 1990s

The widely available mutual fund performance surveys report only the *pretax* total returns of funds. But after-tax return is what counts, and taxes on mutual fund investments can be significant. Further, the tax burdens vary considerably from fund to fund—even among funds that have the same investment goals or style.

A 1993 study computed the after-tax returns of large mutual funds for buy-and-hold investors and compared the after-tax returns with traditional pretax performance rankings. The study, titled *Ranking Mutual Funds on an After-Tax Basis* and prepared by John Shoven and Joel Dickson for the Center for Economic Policy Research of Stanford University, was eye-opening. Some funds with top pretax rankings received mediocre after-tax rankings. Some funds with mediocre pretax performances were at the top of the after-tax performance rankings. On average, taxes ate up 24.22 percent of the total pretax return of a high-tax bracket investor over ten years. Investors in some funds lost more than a third of their returns to taxes.

Tax Wise Mutual Funds

A mutual fund distributes to shareholders most of its interest, dividends, and gains each year. The shareholders are taxed on the distributions. So a mutual fund investor who does not sell any mutual fund shares during the year usually has taxable income from the fund. Tax-deferred compounding is limited for mutual fund investors by the amount of interest, dividends, and net capital gains a fund distributes each year. Usually the amount of the distributions is determined primarily by the fund's investment strategy. A tax wise mutual fund is one whose investment strategy allows investors to defer taxes on as much of the total return as possible. A high-tax mutual fund has little concern for the investor's tax deferral and often leaves the investor with a mediocre after-tax return.

Example. You buy a fund for $10 per share. The fund appreciates by $2 per share this year. In December the fund distributes $1.50 of capital gains to you. You are able to defer taxes on only $0.50 of appreciation this year. The rest is included in your gross income because of the distribution. You also will include in income your share of the dividends and interest earned by the fund.

Note. You do not avoid taxes on distributions by signing up for a fund's dividend reinvestment plan. Under these plans, the fund notifies you of its distributions and uses the distribution to buy you new shares automatically. In this case you still are taxed as though you had received a check for the distribution and wrote a check to the fund to buy the new shares.

Turnover Ratio

One indicator of a fund's likely distributions is its turnover ratio. The turnover ratio is the rate at which a fund buys and sells stocks during the year. A turnover ratio of 100 percent means the fund essentially replaced its entire portfolio during the year. A high turnover ratio means a lot of capital gains are realized, if the fund is successful, and these gains are distributed to shareholders.

Tax wise money strategy. It is difficult to let capital gains compound if you invest in a fund with a high turnover ratio. Instead, when it fits your investment strategy, choose funds with lower turnover ratios so that gains can compound.

Index funds have the lowest turnover ratios, usually under 5 percent. The Stanford study found that *if you take taxes into account, many top-performing funds do not outperform index funds.*

Funds other than index funds have low turnover ratios. In most categories of funds you can find turnover ratios ranging from 25 percent to well over 100 percent. Many studies conclude that the turnover ratio does not affect pretax performance, so when two funds are relatively equal in investment style and pretax returns, choose the one with the lower turnover ratio. The turnover ratio is listed in the prospectus and in some performance surveys.

Another indicator of a fund's likely distributions is its past record of distributions, listed in the prospectus and some mutual fund performance guides. See what percentage of the annual gain in net asset value was distributed to shareholders each year. A fund that regularly distributes more than a third of its appreciation does not give you much tax deferral.

Don't Buy a Tax Bill

If you own the shares on the date of a mutual fund's distributions, you pay the taxes. It doesn't matter how long you owned the shares. Because of this, if you do not plan share purchases carefully you could easily buy someone else's tax bill.

Example. A fund bought a stock two years ago and now has a gain of $5 per mutual fund share. You buy shares in the fund, and one month later the fund sells the stock and makes a distribution of $5 per share. You must include this distribution in your gross income, though the gain was earned before you purchased the shares and it really is a return of your original investment.

Tax wise money strategy. Beware of a fund that lists large unrealized gains in its prospectus. The mutual fund information services from Morningstar, Inc., include an estimate of the unrealized gains of each fund. If the unrealized gains are more than 30 percent of the fund's net asset value per share, examine the past history of distributions. If distributions are fairly level, you probably don't have anything to worry about. But you might want to look at another fund if the fund has a history of making small distributions for several years, then bunching a large distribution in one year.

Beware Year-End Purchases

Another way to buy a tax bill is to invest in a fund just before a distribution.

Example. You invest in Growth Fund, paying $20 per share on December 15. On December 31, Growth Fund makes its year-end distribution of $5 per share. You now have shares worth $15 plus $5 in cash. (If you reinvest distributions, you still have $20 of shares but have more shares than before.) But $5 must be included in gross income for the year. You are taxed for having part of your capital returned to you.

Tax wise money strategy. Check a fund's next distribution date before making an investment. Most mutual fund reporting and ranking services will state how often a fund makes distributions, and most funds will at least give you an estimate of the next distribution date if you call and ask sometime in November. Be especially careful when making investments in late November and December. This is when most funds make their big year-end distributions. If a distribution is coming up, consider delaying your investment until after the distribution.

Tax wise money strategy. If a fund makes a large distribution shortly after you invest, sell the shares immediately. The shares will have declined by an amount equal to the loss, so the distribution and the loss can offset each other on your tax return. To be able to take the loss, you must wait more than thirty days before reinvesting in the fund, or you can invest immediately in a similar fund at another company.

The Retirement Investing Fallacy

Many people are advised that there is a big difference between retirement investing and "accumulation years" investing.

The theory is that you should buy primarily stocks during your working and accumulating years. But at retirement you need to flip the portfolio to reduce sharply or eliminate stocks. Retirees are advised to invest primarily in bonds, utilities, and other income-generating investments.

The tax cost of this strategy is enormous.

Example. You have a stock portfolio worth $500,000, with a tax basis of $250,000. If you sell the stocks to buy an income-producing portfolio, you will pay capital gains taxes of $70,000 on your gain of $250,000. That 14 percent decline in your portfolio's value is greater than the loss experienced in most stock market corrections. And your portfolio will generate 14 percent less income after reinvestment.

Tax wise money strategy. Continue to invest for growth as well as for income after retirement. Use the dividends and interest that your portfolio generates to meet living expenses each year. When the portfolio does not generate enough income to meet expenses, sell some shares of stocks or mutual funds to make up the difference.

This strategy allows you to continue participating in the stock market's growth, giving you some inflation protection. In some years the stocks will not do well and you will be selling principal to meet expenses. But in most years the stock portfolio probably will appreciate even after you take out some living expenses. In addition, you will not lose a big chunk of your capital to a one-time capital gains tax. Another benefit of this approach is that when you sell shares to pay expenses, the gains will be taxed at the maximum capital gains rate of 28 percent instead of the higher top ordinary income tax rates at which interest and dividends are taxed.

Foreign Tax Options

More and more U.S. investors are putting money in international and global stock funds.

Investments in overseas stocks usually are hit with various foreign taxes. These taxes are paid by the fund and reduce net asset value. But U.S.

shareholders can report the taxes on their own tax returns and get a tax benefit from them.

You have two options for handling the foreign taxes paid. One option is to claim the foreign taxes as a credit, using Form 1116. A tax credit is valuable, because $1 of tax credit reduces $1 of your U.S. income tax bill. But Form 1116 is very complicated, because there are limits on your foreign tax credit that must be computed. Often the amount of the credit is not worth the time it takes to work through the form or to pay a tax preparer to complete the form.

The other option is to take a deduction for the foreign taxes paid. While this is not as valuable as a credit, taking the deduction is easier and does not take a lot of time or greatly increase your tax preparation fee.

Tax wise money strategy. If your share of foreign taxes paid by the mutual fund is not a lot of money, take the deduction on Schedule A as an itemized expense on the "Other Taxes" line.

Getting Taxed Twice

Most mutual funds offer a dividend reinvestment plan. Under the plan, you are told of distributions but not sent a check. Instead the fund automatically buys you additional shares with the distribution. The amount of the distribution is your tax basis in the new shares.

Most people get into trouble because they do not keep good records of their reinvested distributions and so do not know the tax basis for the shares. When you do not know your tax basis, the basis is considered to be zero, and you will pay taxes on your principal instead of only on your gains. Most funds will generate the records for you, but it might cost a few dollars and often takes months to get the paperwork.

Tax wise money strategy. Keep a record of your initial investment, reinvested distributions, and sales of mutual fund shares. You need this information to ensure that you pay the right amount of tax and no more when you sell the shares. A simple notebook that you update once or twice a year is sufficient to save you from quite a headache when shares are sold.

Surprise Redemptions

Many mutual funds offer check-writing privileges. Instead of calling up the fund to redeem shares and mail a check, you simply write a check against your fund account. When the check is presented to the fund, it cashes out your shares.

The problem with check-writing privileges is that every time you write a check against your fund shares you have a sale that must be reported on your tax return. This is not a problem with a money market fund, because most money market funds maintain a constant share value of $1. But stock and bond funds have fluctuating share values, so you will have a capital gain or loss.

Tax wise money strategy. Do not use a stock or bond fund as a checking account. Sales of your mutual funds should be carefully considered as part of your tax and investment plans and not be part of your monthly bill-paying routine.

Don't Overpay When Selling Shares

There are several options for computing gains and losses when you sell mutual fund shares, and your choice affects your tax bill.

Mutual fund shares are capital assets, so you compute the gain or loss by subtracting your tax basis in the shares (usually your original cost) from the amount realized on the sale. But with mutual funds, when you sell less than your complete holdings in a fund, you can choose from four ways of computing your basis:

First-in, First-out Method
This is the method the IRS prefers and is used if you do not select another option. Under FIFO, as it is known, you assume that the first shares you bought were the first ones sold. If the shares appreciated while you held them, this method maximizes the amount of tax you pay, because the first shares you bought probably will have the lowest basis.

Single-Category Method
This is a simple averaging method. You add up your total investment in the fund and divide it by the number of shares you owned immediately before the sale. The result is your basis in each share sold. To determine if you have short-term or long-term gains or losses, you assume that the first shares you bought were the first ones sold.

Several mutual fund companies have started computing the basis of shares sold and putting this on shareholder statements. The computation is an average, usually using the single-category method.

Double-Category Method

This is another averaging method. The difference is that first you divide your shares into short-term shares (those held for one year or less) and long-term shares (those held for more than one year). Then you compute the average basis for each group of shares and assume the shares were sold in the order they were purchased.

Specific-Identification Method

This method gives you the maximum flexibility for reducing taxes, because you can choose to sell the shares with the highest basis, and that either minimizes gain or maximizes losses. To use this method, before the sale you must specifically identify the shares to be sold and get a written confirmation from the fund company or broker that those were the shares sold. Not all fund companies will provide the needed written confirmation.

Once you use a method for a fund, you usually have to use that same method for the rest of your shares. You also must state on your return when you are using one of the category methods.

Tax wise money strategy. The specific-identification method usually is the best, since it gives you the most control over your tax burden. If you do not qualify for that method, then at tax return time compute the taxes under each of the other methods and choose the one that gives the best result. If your mutual fund will not cooperate with the specific identification method, consider investing your mutual funds through a broker.

Using Interest to Shelter Dividend and Interest Income

One way to shelter dividends and interest from mutual funds (or other investments) is to take an itemized deduction for interest paid to purchase or carry investments. The interest is deductible only to the extent of your net investment income for the year. Net investment income includes interest, dividends, and royalties. (Under the 1993 tax hike, net investment income does not include long-term capital gains.) Any investment interest that you pay but cannot deduct this year because of the limit is carried forward indefinitely to future years until you can deduct it.

Example. Max Profits buys stocks on margin. That means he pays cash for about half the cost of his stocks and borrows the other half. In 1995 he pays interest on his margin account of $10,000. He earned interest income of $2,000 and dividends of $5,000, for net investment income of $7,000. Max can shelter the $7,000 of interest and dividends with the investment interest expense deduction. The other $3,000 of investment interest is carried forward to next year.

You can choose to include long-term capital gains in net investment income. The price for this is that the capital gains will be taxed at the same rate as your other income, which could be as high as 39.6 percent, instead of the maximum capital gains rate of 28 percent.

Tax wise money strategy. Making the election to include long-term capital gains in net investment income makes sense if you have a lot of investment interest expense to deduct and you will not be in either the 36 percent or the 39.6 percent tax bracket for the year. But in the higher tax brackets the cost of having your long-term capital gains taxed as ordinary income is too high unless you have enough investment interest expense to shelter the capital gains.

Example. Max Profits in the previous example has long-term capital gains for the year of $5,000, and he is in the 31 percent tax bracket. If he elects to include capital gains in net investment income, his investment interest expense for the year is increased by $3,000. That reduces his taxes by $930. His capital gains will be taxed at a 3 percent higher rate (31 percent instead of 28 percent), which costs him $150 in taxes. Max comes out ahead making the election.

Key point. You can elect to include *all or part* of your long-term capital gains in net investment income for the year. So you can give up the maximum 28 percent tax rate for just enough capital gains to be offset by your investment interest, and allow the rest of your capital gains to be taxed at the favorable 28 percent rate.

Tax Wise Debt Management

When you borrow money, the *use* of the loan proceeds determines whether the interest paid is investment interest. If you borrow against your investment portfolio and use the loan proceeds to buy a car, the interest is not investment interest. But if you use the loan proceeds to buy more stocks—or bonds or mutual funds—the interest you pay is investment interest.

Tax wise money strategy. Suppose you have $10,000. You would like to buy a car and also invest in some mutual funds. You could use $2,000 as a down payment on the car, borrow the rest of the car's purchase price, and invest the other $8,000. If you do this, none of the interest of the car loan will be deductible. A tax wise strategy is to put $4,000 in mutual funds in a brokerage account and borrow another $4,000 from the broker to buy more funds. That still leaves you with $8,000 in the funds. The interest you pay on that loan is deductible to the extent of net investment income. Then you have $6,000 to make a larger down payment on the car and reduce your nondeductible interest payments.

Caution. When money is borrowed to buy investments, you are liable for a "margin call" if the value of the investments falls too far. That means you must find cash from other sources to make up for the decline in the value of the investments, or the broker will sell enough investments to cover the outstanding loan.

Stocks or Mutual Funds?

Will mutual funds or individual stocks do a better job of lowering your tax bill?

Buying individual stocks gives you more control over the timing and tax consequences of your investments. With a portfolio of individual stocks you can:

- Let your gains compound for years before you sell and incur capital gains taxes; you do not have to sell when a stock stumbles in order to please outside analysts, and you do not have to sell stocks to redeem the shares of departing investors;
- sell losing investments to shelter capital gains you already took this year;
- avoid purchasing hidden tax liabilities by buying into a mutual fund that has unrealized capital gains;
- avoid high commissions that result when a mutual fund actively trades a large number of stocks.

Of course, there are advantages to investing through mutual funds. You do not have to follow the stocks of individual companies, and the mutual fund handles the buying and selling of stocks. The mutual fund is a fast, easy way to get a diversified portfolio.

In addition, most stock investors do not take advantage of their tax reduction opportunities. Instead of buying stocks for long-term gains and letting the gains compound tax-deferred for years, individual stock owners buy and sell too frequently. So while the investor in individual stocks *should* be in a better tax position because of the flexibility available, most stock investors do not take advantage of their tax planning opportunities. In addition, many individual investors feel they do not have the time to locate, research, and follow a portfolio of individual stocks. The tax advantages do little good if you cannot ensure that good stocks are in your portfolio.

How to Invest in Deferred Accounts

The standard advice after the 1993 tax law changes is that stock market investments should be in taxable accounts and that income investments such as bonds should be in tax-deferred accounts. The rationale is that stocks have a maximum tax rate of 28 percent, while interest and dividend income could be taxed as high as 39.6 percent. In addition, when stocks are put in a deferred account, withdrawals eventually will be taxed as ordinary income. You would lose the benefit of the 28 percent maximum tax rate on capital gains. So it makes sense that interest and dividends should be given the advantage of tax deferral.

But this intuitive answer is not always correct.

Tax wise money strategy. My research indicates that the benefits of tax-deferred accounts are maximized when investments with the highest expected returns are in the tax-deferred accounts. Even the higher tax on gains when they are withdrawn from the tax-deferred account does not hurt—if the gains are allowed to compound long enough.

There are a couple of exceptions. One is when you do not plan to leave the money in the tax-deferred account for a number of years. Then, if you are in a top bracket, you might as well leave the equities outside the tax-deferred account and take advantage of the 28 percent maximum capital gains rate.

The second exception is when your mutual fund will let you achieve tax-deferred compounding in a taxable account. If you make few sales of funds and invest in tax wise mutual funds that make low distributions each year, a taxable account would give you the best of both worlds: tax-deferred compounding plus the maximum 28 percent tax rate when you finally sell. This also is true if you buy a few individual stocks and hold them for years.

Investment Recordkeeping Work Sheet

Name of asset   Account number

Address   Telephone

Name asset held in   Account rep./Other information

Purchase and Sale Record

Date	Description	Total Value	Price Per Unit	Total No. of Units	Total Units Owned

Chapter 6

Creating Your Own Capital Gains Tax Cut: How to Bypass Congress

Americans have accumulated an estimated $7 trillion in unrealized capital gains. They would like Congress to cut the tax rate on long-term capital gains so they can sell their appreciated property and reinvest the bulk of their after-tax profits in something else.

But you do not have to wait for politicians to cut your capital gains taxes. There already are many ways to cut capital gains taxes right in the tax code. We'll start with the basics and work up to some more advanced tax wise money strategies for investors with long-term large capital gains.

The Cost of Capital Gains Taxes

Look at how the 28 percent tax on long-term gains affects after-tax wealth and why you need to reduce capital gains taxes whenever possible.

Example. Max Profits has a stock portfolio worth about $500,000 that has cost about $250,000 over the years. Max wants to sell the stocks and invest his portfolio to yield about 5 percent annually, giving him a pretax annual income of about $25,000. But Max has a long-term capital gains of $250,000 and a sale would mean a tax bill of $70,000—14 percent of Max's retirement fund—and bring his portfolio down to $430,000. Invested to yield 5 percent, the portfolio would yield $21,500 annually before taxes—a 14 percent cut in Max's retirement income. Unless Max lives in one of the few states that do not tax capital gains, the loss will be higher when state capital gains taxes are paid.

Here are some ways Max could avoid losing his wealth to capital gains taxes.

Turning Losses into Assets

You can get a tax benefit from an investment loss. A realized capital loss can offset capital gains on a dollar-for-dollar basis. In addition, when your capital losses for the year exceed your capital gains, up to $3,000 of the excess losses can be deducted against other income. The rest of the losses can be carried forward to future years until they are used up.

Tax wise money strategy. Recognize any paper capital losses in the same year you realize capital gains. In other words, match your capital gains with capital losses.

Example. Suppose you have a $10,000 gain in some mutual fund shares, which in the 28 percent tax bracket costs you $2,800 in taxes. You have other mutual fund investments that you are just hanging on to until the day when they appreciate enough to let you break even. Instead of hanging on, you should sell these investments until you realize $10,000 of losses to offset your gains for the year, or until you have no more unrealized losses left.

The result is extraordinary. Your capital gain will not be taxed, and you have taken your capital out of the losing investment and are able to invest it more profitably. Even putting the proceeds in a money market fund would be better than leaving the money in a losing investment.

Wash Sales—Having Your Cake and Eating It, Too

Many times an investor does not want to sell losing investments because the investments are only temporarily depressed and still are good long-term investments.

The solution to this dilemma is in the tax code's "wash sale" rules— or actually in avoiding the wash sale rules.

If you buy a security within thirty days of selling a "substantially identical" asset at a loss, this is considered a wash sale and you cannot deduct the loss. Instead, you defer the loss by adding it to the tax basis of the substantially identical asset you bought.

Example. You sell mutual fund shares at a loss on August 1, then buy shares in the same fund after September 1. (When counting thirty days, you do count the days you sell one block and buy the other block as full days. But play it safe and leave a few days' room.) Since your transactions were not within thirty days of each other, the wash sale rules do not apply. You get to deduct the loss from your August 1 sale.

If your repurchase of the shares were on August 15, you would not deduct the loss from the August 1 sale. Instead you would add the loss to the basis of the shares you purchased on August 15. In effect, the August 1 loss would be taken when you sell the August 15 shares.

Of course, the investment could appreciate sharply while you are out of the market, especially if it is a volatile asset. Fortunately, there is ways you can take the loss to shelter your gain, avoid the wash sale rules, and stay in the market.

Tax wise money strategy. Sell your losing shares as planned, and simultaneously buy shares in a mutual fund with a similar investment style from a different fund company. The thirty-day waiting period will not apply because the funds are not "substantially identical" under the tax rules. The definition of substantially identical leaves room for you to invest in the same type of mutual fund at another fund family.

This strategy is easier to do with mutual funds than with stocks. In mutual funds, you could, for example, sell United Services Gold Shares while buying Lexington Strategic Investment or any of several other gold stock mutual funds. With stocks and bonds, different companies in the same industry are not always in the same financial and market positions. In addition, you never know what surprises might come out of a company that would affect the performance of its stock. Nevertheless, brokerage firms are willing to offer advice in these situations and try to match you to a stock or bond that will meet your requirements.

Doubling up. An alternative if you have the cash is to buy additional shares of the losing investment more than thirty days before you plan to sell the original shares. You will have a double exposure in the investment for a while, but after the sale you will be able to recognize the loss without being out of the market.

Identifying Shares

When you plan to sell part but not all of an investment in a stock, bond, or mutual fund, you could do as most investors do and ask your broker or fund to sell the appropriate number of shares at the market price. The result is that the first shares you bought will be considered to be the first ones sold. Most of the time, those shares were bought at the lowest prices, which means that they will have the biggest taxable capital gains.

Tax wise money strategy. A better strategy, which the IRS allows, is to "earmark" or specifically identify the shares you want to sell. Instead of telling your broker or fund to sell just a certain number of shares, specifically identify the shares you want to sell. Get out your purchase records and sell the shares that cost you the most money. In that way you either minimize taxable gains or maximize losses.

The IRS says that for earmarking shares to be effective, your broker must give you written confirmation that it sold the shares you designated. Because of the tax dollars at stake it is worthwhile to demand correct confirmation statements from the broker, or to search for a broker who will work with you on this strategy. Not all mutual funds will give the right confirmation for this strategy to work, so you might want to trade your mutual fund shares through a broker or deal only with funds that will help you cut taxes.

Use the Family Device

The family device is so important that I have devoted a full chapter to it. With the family device you shift income or capital gains to a family member who is in a lower tax bracket than you are, usually a child or grandchild. In that way the income or gain remains in the family, but the tax burden is reduced. This increases the family's after-tax wealth.

Example. A parent has mutual fund shares worth $20,000, with a taxable gain of $10,000. At a 28 percent tax rate, the tax is $2,800, leaving after-tax proceeds of $17,200. Instead of selling, the parent gives the shares to his two teenagers in the 15 percent tax bracket. Each child incurs a $5,000 taxable gain. The total tax is $1,500. That's a savings of $1,300, or 6.5 percent of the total value of the shares.

You have to avoid gift taxes and the kiddie tax to use the family device successfully.

Reverse Family Device Eliminates Capital Gains

With the family device a parent gives property to a child or grandchild. But sometimes an adult finds it beneficial to transfer property to his or her parent. For example, an adult child helping support a parent might find that the parent is in a lower tax bracket. Then it is wise to give appreciated property to the parent. You still have to avoid gift taxes, but do not have to worry about the kiddie tax.

In addition, giving appreciated property to a parent could completely eliminate capital gains taxes and eventually get the property to your children. Here's how it works.

Example. You give property to your parent. There might be gift taxes on this transfer, depending on the value of the property at the time of the transfer. Your parent holds the property and provides in his or her will that the property will pass to your child or to a trust for the child's benefit.

At your parent's death, the tax basis of the property increases to its fair market value. That means your child or the trust can sell it immediately and pay no capital gains taxes. If the property is not sold immediately after the inheritance, there might be some capital gain, but it won't be taxed at your rate if the child is age fourteen or older by that time.

This strategy takes a while to work, but it completely eliminates capital gains on the property. To make this approach most effective, your parent should not have a large taxable estate or should have adequate life insurance or other means to pay the estate taxes. Otherwise the estate taxes might exceed the capital gains taxes you were trying to avoid.

Donation to Charity

The tax law gives you a charitable contribution deduction for the fair market value of long-term capital gains property that you donate to a charity. There is no tax on the appreciation that occurred before the contribution. Details are in the chapter on charitable giving.

Triple Tax Reduction

Let's return to the sad case of Max Profits that started this chapter. Max wants to change his portfolio without substantially decreasing his retirement income.

One possible solution is the triple tax reduction tactic. This strategy will allow Max to avoid capital gains taxes, take a charitable deduction this year, receive income for life, and avoid estate taxes on the property. The strategy is also known as the charitable remainder trust.

Tax wise money strategy. Instead of selling his stock, Max sets up an irrevocable charitable trust and transfers the stock to the trust. That gives Max an income-tax deduction equal to the present value of the charitable gift, based on the current value of the stock, $500,000, current interest rates and Max's life expectancy. Charitable contribution deductions are limited to no more than 50 percent of adjusted gross income each year, but unused deductions can be carried forward to future years. So Max might have to stretch out the deduction for several years. Max also has to avoid the itemized deduction reduction for high-income taxpayers.

After the contribution, the charitable trust sells the stocks. Since this is a charitable trust, its capital gains are exempt from tax, and the entire $500,000 in sale proceeds is reinvested to yield 5 percent, just as Max planned. This produces $25,000 of annual income, which is not taxed to the trust.

Under its terms, the trust pays income to Max and his wife, Rosie, for the rest of their lives. The tax law gives Max flexibility in setting the amount of income to be paid annually. Max chose to have 4 percent of the trust's assets paid to him. So he gets $20,000 this year, and $5,000 is reinvested by the trust. The reinvestment will increase next year's trust income, and next year's payment to Max. This approach gives Max some inflation protection. Max and Rosie are taxed on the payout each year.

After Max and his wife die, the trust property will be paid to charity as designated by Max when he set up the trust, and there will be no estate taxes.

A potential disadvantage to the charitable remainder trust is that the Profits' children will not inherit the property held in the trust. But this might not be as big a problem as it at first appears.

Tax wise money strategy. Max could set up an irrevocable life insurance trust, sometimes called a wealth replacement trust, and give some of the tax savings and increased income he gets from the charitable trust to the insurance trust. The insurance trust uses the money to buy life insurance. Instead of inheriting property, his heirs inherit the life insurance benefits.

The charitable trust provides great flexibility. You can, within limits, determine the amount of income to be paid each year, and it can be a fixed amount or a fluctuating amount that provides some inflation protection.

A charitable trust is ideal for someone who has substantially appreciated property and plans to live off the income from that property. It is especially appropriate when the property is not generating enough income, is unlikely to appreciate further, or for some other reason needs to be sold and reinvested. If you also are inclined toward charitable giving anyway, the charitable trust definitely should be carefully considered.

Let Your Heirs Inherit

The ultimate way to avoid capital gains taxes is to let your heirs inherit property. When property is inherited, the heirs get to increase the tax basis to the fair market value at the time of death. That means the property can be sold immediately, no capital gains taxes will be due, and the appreciation that occurred during your lifetime will never face income taxes.

If your will leaves the property to your spouse, the marital deduction avoids any state taxes on the property at your death, and your spouse gets to increase the tax basis to fair market value. If you leave the property to other heirs, you have to be wary that estate taxes do not take away all the capital gains tax savings.

Take Tax-Free or Tax-Deferred Gain on Your Home

Individuals age fifty-five or over are allowed, once, to take $125,000 of capital gains on their principal residence tax-free. All home sellers can defer taxes on the gain by purchasing a new home at the same or higher price within two years. Details of these strategies are in the chapter on home equity.

Borrow Against an Asset

Instead of selling or giving away an asset, consider borrowing against it. This allows you access to at least a portion of the appreciation, and loan proceeds are not taxable. If the asset is a first or second residence and secures the loan, the interest might be deductible as qualified home mortgage interest. Other loans might generate deductible interest if the proceeds are used for business or investment purposes.

A disadvantage to borrowing against an asset is that you must repay the loan plus interest. In addition, many people who borrow against assets have ended up in bankruptcy court after asset values declined or sources of income to repay the loan dried up. So this strategy must be used carefully.

Sell Passive Loss Activities

The passive loss rules of tax reform effectively shut down most tax shelters. These rules provide that in most cases losses from passive activities can be deducted only against income from passive activities. Unused losses are suspended until there is enough passive income generated for them to offset.

A passive activity generally is one in which you do not materially participate. Passive activities are meant to include tax shelters and other investment activities but exclude your main business.

Tax wise money strategy. Passive activity losses can be deducted against any type of income when the passive activity is disposed of. If you have large capital gains that you would like to realize without capital gains taxes and also own some passive activities that are generating losses you have not been able to use, consider selling passive activities to realize the accumulated suspended losses in the same year you have capital gains. The losses might shelter your capital gains from taxes.

One reason why some passive activity owners do not sell is that they have large debts on the passive activities. When the activities are sold, any debt that is assumed by the buyer or that is written off by the lender is treated as cash you recieve for the sale of the asset. When the tax basis of the asset is less than the debt, instead of a loss there is a substantial gain.

Like-Kind Exchange

The tax law allows owners of business or investment property to exchange the property for like-kind business or investment property. No taxes are due unless you receive property other than real estate in the exchange. This is known as a tax-deferred or like-kind exchange and is especially popular among real-estate owners.

The price you pay is that the tax basis of the new property is the same as the tax basis of your old property. The effect of this is to defer taxes until you sell the new property. If you want to cash out your real estate investments, the like-kind exchange is not for you. But if you want to sell a particular piece of real estate and buy another, the like-kind exchange increases your purchasing power.

The like-kind exchange can be used only for business or investment property and cannot be used for stocks, bonds, or mutual funds. There are many qualifications that must be met to have an effective tax-deferred exchange. You should consult an experienced tax adviser before attempting one of these.

Contribute to a Business

Contributing property to a corporation or partnership in return for an ownership interest is a tax-free transaction. You receive your ownership interest based on the value of the property you contributed, but you do not have to pay capital gains taxes on appreciation in the property you contributed. This is a good way to shift your portfolio without dilution from capital gains taxes. The price for this deferral is that your tax basis in the new ownership interest is the same as your tax basis in the property you exchanged.

There are special rules for partnerships that eliminate the tax deferral if the partnership sells the property within two years of your contribution.

This is known as a "disguised sale." The tax rules are fairly complicated, so get good tax advice if you might be in this situation.

Spreading Out the Taxes

If you cannot avoid capital gains taxes, you might be able to spread them out over several years by making an installment sale. You pay taxes only as the payments are actually received. Each payment will be divided into a tax-free return of capital, taxable interest, and capital gains. By spreading the gain over several years, you also might reduce your income enough each year to avoid tax penalties such as the phaseout of personal exemptions and the itemized-deduction reduction. Installment sales cannot be used for sales of publicly traded property such as stocks and bonds.

Chapter 7

Tax-Deferred Investing Through Insurance: Best-Selling Tax Shelter of the 1990s

Tax-deferred compounding of income and gains is the second most powerful tax wise money strategy (after earning tax-free income). And the higher tax rates imposed by the 1993 law make tax deferral more powerful than it has been since 1986.

The most popular and effective tax-deferral vehicles in recent years have been insurance products, including fixed annuities, variable annuities, whole life insurance, and variable life insurance. In this chapter you will learn how to analyze these products and find the true costs and benefits of tax deferral. Other tax-deferral strategies discussed elsewhere in this book include qualified retirement plans, nonqualified deferred compensation, and tax shelters.

Traps in Tax Deferral

Tax deferral usually comes with costs and restrictions. For example, a tax cost is that any capital gains earned by your deferred account are taxed as ordinary income when you withdraw the money. Other nontax costs are the restrictions and additional expenses imposed on your account by the insurance companies.

In addition, you need to examine closely any illustrations of the benefits of tax deferral, because the illustrations often do not account for all the additional costs or restrictions, or they assume unrealistically high returns. You will learn examples of how to make this examination in this chapter.

Fixed Annuities

The fixed annuity is the basic, traditional tax-deferred annuity. You give money to an insurance company, your account is credited with interest each year, and the interest income compounds tax-deferred until you take withdrawals.

Fixed annuities fell out of favor in the 1970s and early 1980s because their yields really were fixed at about 3 percent or 4 percent. After inflation and taxes, investors were losing money. But now most fixed annuities yield about the same as intermediate bonds and have interest rates that rise and fall with market rates. Annuities also have the advantage over bonds that the principal value does not fluctuate as interest rates rise and fall.

Tax wise money strategy. Fixed annuities are a tax wise alternative for the bond or fixed-income portion of your investment portfolio. If your investment income is more than you need to meet expenses for the next few years, consider putting some of your portfolio in a fixed annuity so the interest can compound tax-deferred. This is a particularly good idea if you have a lot of money sitting in certificates of deposit or money market funds.

Choosing a Fixed Annuity

Here are some features you want to examine before choosing an annuity.

Surrender penalties. Most annuities charge a penalty for cashing out early. The standard penalty is 7 percent of your account the first year, and it declines by a percentage point each year, so there is no penalty after seven years. But some have penalties for as long as fifteen years. Often you can avoid the surrender penalty by withdrawing 10 percent to 15 percent of your account each year instead of taking the entire account.

The tax law also imposes a surrender penalty. If you withdraw money before age 59½ you pay income taxes plus an early distribution penalty of 10 percent of the amount withdrawn. The chapter on retirement plan distributions describes several ways to avoid this penalty.

Hidden surrender penalties. A market value adjustment occurs when you withdraw from the annuity early and your entire account balance is recalculated as though you earned a lower interest rate from the start. You will be paid the lower, recalculated account balance. This is a disguised surrender penalty

Yield calculations and expenses. The "gross yield" is not what is credited to your account, though it might be used in sales materials. Fees and expenses are subtracted from the gross yield to arrive at the net yield—the yield actually credited to your account.

Always ask for the yield net of all expenses. Also, ask for a complete list of the expenses that will be deducted from the gross yield or account balance, and ask which ones can be changed during the life of the annuity. (Most states charge a premium tax on annuity deposits; be sure this is included in your calculations.)

Guaranteed yield. Most fixed annuities offer a guaranteed interest rate, currently about 4 percent.

Yield reset. The initial yield usually is guaranteed for one year or less. After that the yield is reset, and the reset method varies greatly. You'll find that insurers offering the greatest initial yields usually make up for it by paying below-average yields after the first year.

Your preference should be for a yield reset that is based on some intermediate bond market index, such as the yield on five-year or ten-year Treasuries. An annuity is an intermediate to long-term investment, and you should earn a comparable yield. You definitely do not want a yield that is based on either a short-term investment, such as money funds, or on a tax-exempt yield.

Some annuity resets are based on the insurer's investment experience. This is fine if the insurer has a good investment record that is likely to continue. You should be able to get information on the past investment experience of the insurer from the agent or broker. In addition, you should check the insurer's current portfolio as listed in the credit rating report.

Tax wise money strategy. No matter how the yield is recalculated, ask for the renewal rate history of annuities offered by the insurer. This will tell you if the insurer treats its annuity holders fairly all the time, or only for the first year. A good renewal rate history will show the yield on the insurer's fixed annuities moving up and down with changes in intermediate or long-term interest rates. A bad renewal history will show a sharp drop after the first year or so that is not matched by a similar change in market interest rates.

Beware of bonus points. Some annuities add bonus points to your yield when the insurer's actual investment returns exceed what it projected when yields were reset. Do not let the past record of bonus points influence your choice of an annuity. Bonus points are not guaranteed and could end the year you sign up. In addition, many bonus points are withdrawn if you take the annuity payout in a lump sum or over a shorter period than the insurer wants you to.

Safety. A high yield does little good if the insurer fails. You should check the safety ratings of all five major services: A. M. Best, S&P, Moody's, Duff & Phelps, and Weiss Research. Another good step is to look at the composition of the insurer's investment portfolio. You might decide that even a top-rated insurer owns too many mortgages or high-yield bonds for your comfort.

Withdrawal options. This critical provision is discussed later in this chapter.

The Offshore Advantage

Many Americans want to diversify their investments internationally to hedge against a long-term decline in the value of the dollar, to take advantage of growth outside the United States, or because interest rates are higher in other countries. If you want to diversify investments internationally, one way is through a foreign annuity, especially a Swiss annuity.

Many Swiss insurers have structured their annuities to qualify for deferral under U.S. tax laws, and they have the same withdrawal restrictions and other tax consequences as U.S. annuities. But the annuities are not registered for sale with any state in the United States. You have to go through a Swiss broker to buy them.

Swiss annuities basically are a bet that the dollar will decline in value against the Swiss franc, because yields are not great on Swiss annuities. There also are assertions that assets in Swiss annuities are protected from the claims of U.S. creditors, but that has not been tested in court, and not everyone agrees that this protection will stand up.

Variable Annuities

Variable annuities have been the best-selling insurance products in recent years. In a variable annuity, the insurer offers different investment funds, and you choose how your account is invested among them. A variable annuity might offer as little as three or as many as several dozen investment options. The value of your account rises and falls with the performance of these investments, but it has a death benefit so that the value to your beneficiary will not be less than your contributions.

The variable annuity effectively is a tax-deferred way to invest in the mutual funds provided by the insurer. But a variable annuity is not quite the same as investing in mutual funds through an IRA or other retirement account. There are some important differences to consider.

Price of Deferral

You pay for a variable annuity's tax deferral and investment flexibility through a range of fees subtracted from your account.

The insurance company charges an annual fee for maintaining the account. This fee, which is subtracted from your account's return, usually ranges from 0.5 percent to 2 percent of assets each year. The fund also will charge an additional fee of about 1.5 percent annually to pay for the death benefit and administrative expenses. Another charge is an annual maintenance free of $30 or so. These fees total more than the typical mutual fund's annual management expenses. The average variable annuity's fees are about 2.1 percent.

Because of these expenses, *a mutual fund in a variable annuity actually will have a lower pretax return after all expenses than the identical mutual fund in a taxable account.*

Costs differ greatly from one variable annuity to the other. So it pays to compare the expenses of different annuities.

How much does it pay to compare costs? I took a list of the top-performing variable annuity equity subaccounts over a three-year period and discovered that fourteen of the top fifteen investment accounts were actually the same mutual fund offered through the variable annuities of different insurers. But the average annual three-year returns ranged from 21.65 percent to 20.9 percent. This difference was due solely to different fees charged by each of the annuities. That 0.75 percent difference seems small. But a $50,000 initial investment (about average for variable annuities) over three years in the highest-performing fund this would have compounded to $90,013, while in the lower-performing fund it would total only $88,359. That difference is equal to more than 3 percent of the initial investment. The level of expenses will greatly determine whether an annuity is a good deal for you.

Surrender charges. Variable annuities usually impose surrender charges similar to those imposed on fixed annuities. But with variable annuities it usually is ten years or longer before the surrender charge disappears.

Inflexibility

Another disadvantage to variable annuities is that you are limited to the investment accounts or mutual funds that are affiliated with the annuity (known as subaccounts). The tax deferral does little good if the mutual funds offered in the annuity substantially underperform the market averages or the average mutual fund.

Some variable annuities now offer more than two dozen investment options and offer mutual funds from a number of different fund management companies. But most variable annuities still offer five to seven investment options, and most of those are funds managed by the same organization.

Tax Penalties

Variable annuities have the same tax penalties as fixed annuities: an early distribution penalty for withdrawals before age 59½ equal to 10 percent of the amount withdrawn.

In addition, the capital gains earned by your account all will be taxed as ordinary income when you withdraw them instead of being taxed at the maximum twenty-eight percent long-term capital gains rate. This is a big difference to someone in the 36 percent or 39.6 percent tax bracket.

How Much You'll Really Get

Most proposals for variable annuities show the different amounts you would have in a variable annuity account and a taxable mutual fund account over time, assuming the same rate of return. The proposals make an impressive case for variable annuities but do that by ignoring some key points.

A realistic comparison of variable annuities and taxable mutual funds assumes that some taxable mutual fund returns can be deferred, and that some of the annual taxable distributions from a fund are taxed at a maximum 28 percent rate while distributions from an annuity are taxed as ordinary income. The more realistic analysis also takes into account the extra fees incurred by a variable annuity, so that the annuity has a lower pretax return.

Example. You have $25,000 to invest. You could put it in no-load mutual funds with annual expenses of 1 percent, that distribute 30 percent of annual appreciation to shareholders as ordinary income (dividends and interest), and 30 percent as capital gains. The other 30 percent of appreciation is unrealized capital gains, so it is not taxed at that point. You estimate that each year you would sell about 25 percent of the mutual fund shares, pay taxes, and buy shares in other funds.

You also are considering both a low-cost variable annuity with annual fees of 1.5 percent and an average-cost annuity with annual expenses of 2.1 percent. Your combined federal-state income-tax rate is 32 percent during the accumulation phase of your investments, and you assume that it will be the same when you start to spend the money.

Charts 1 and 2 show the most favorable aspect of the variable annuities: the pretax, preliquidation account balances. Since the annuities have not incurred any taxes yet, their balances are much higher than for the mutual fund account.

But what counts is the amount of money you keep after taxes—your after-tax wealth. Tables 1 and 2 present your possible after-tax wealth in two ways.

The first set of figures in each table shows the after-tax cash left after liquidating each of the accounts in a lump sum. The second set of figures in each table shows the after-tax payments you could get by converting the variable annuities into immediate annuities and using the taxable account to buy an immediate annuity.

Tax wise money strategy. There are two conclusions to draw from these figures. One conclusion is that the higher the rate of return you earn, the better a variable annuity looks. That's because a high return leverages the advantage of tax deferral. The second conclusion is that a variable annuity needs a long time for the power of tax deferral to overcome clearly the higher costs of the annuity. Most investors need to let the returns compound for at least fifteen years to come out clearly ahead with the variable annuity.

High-bracket investor. What if you are in one of the new higher tax brackets of 36 percent or 39.6 percent? I did not include a chart or tables, but the results are not encouraging for high-bracket investors. That's because the tax rate on capital gains is capped at 28 percent in taxable accounts, but all distributions from an annuity are taxed as ordinary income. So if you will continue to be in the upper tax bracket after withdrawals from the annuity begin, you actually are increasing your tax rate substantially on any capital gains earned by the annuity account. Unless you expect to be in a lower tax bracket when taking distributions, a high-bracket taxpayer loses money in a variable annuity.

Assumptions. You can make either investment option look more or less attractive by changing the assumptions. To make variable annuities look more attractive, you could assume that a greater percentage of the mutual funds would be sold each year or that there would be higher taxable annual distributions from the funds. You could make the opposite changes to make mutual funds more attractive than the variable annuity.

How to Pick a Variable Annuity

Variable annuities are not winners for everyone. But they can be powerful tax and retirement planning tools for the right individuals. Here are some rules to consider when looking at variable annuities.

• A variable annuity should be considered only after you have exhausted other tax-deferral vehicles with lower costs. These include employer pension plans, 401(k)s, IRAs (even nondeductible ones), tax wise mutual funds, and nonqualified deferred compensation plans.

• For tax deferral to offset the higher costs and other disadvantages,

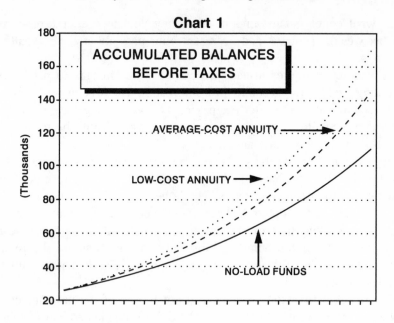

Chart 1

ACCUMULATED BALANCES BEFORE TAXES

AVERAGE-COST ANNUITY

LOW-COST ANNUITY

NO-LOAD FUNDS

Table 1
Liquidation Value After Taxes and Fees

Tax Rate: 32%   Rate of Return: 8%

Years Compounded	No-Load Fund	Low-Cost Variable Ann.	Average Cost Variable Ann.
5	31,747	31,161	30,579
10	40,367	39,554	37,988
15	51,333	50,988	47,829
20	65,280	66,566	60,899
25	83,016	87,790	78,258
30	105,570	116,705	101,313

Annual Annuity After Taxes and Fees

Tax Rate: 32%   Rate of Return: 8%

Years Compounded	No-Load Fund	Low-Cost Variable Ann.	Average Cost Variable Ann.
5	2,707	2,759	2,700
10	3,442	3,614	3,454
15	4,377	4,778	4,457
20	5,566	6,365	5,788
25	7,078	8,527	7.556
30	9,001	11,472	9,904

Chart 2

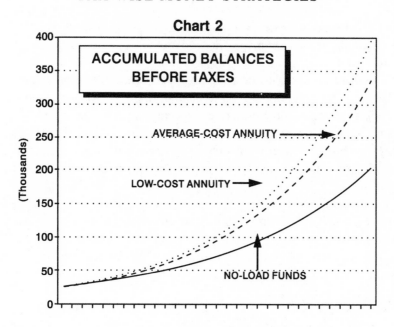

ACCUMULATED BALANCES BEFORE TAXES

AVERAGE-COST ANNUITY →

LOW-COST ANNUITY →

NO-LOAD FUNDS

Table 2
Liquidation Value After Taxes and Fees

	Tax Rate: 32%		Rate of Return: 11%
Years Compounded	No-Load Fund	Low-Cost Variable Ann.	Average-Cost Variable Ann.
5	35,015	34,561	33,894
10	49,199	49,499	47,440
15	69,150	72,839	68,074
20	97,195	109,306	99,502
25	136,614	166,281	147,372
30	192,021	255,301	220,286

Annual Annuity After Taxes and Fees

	Tax Rate: 32%		Rate of Return: 11%
Years Compounded	No-Load Fund	Low-Cost Variable Ann.	Average-Cost Variable Ann.
5	3,550	3,735	3,652
10	4,988	5,611	5,353
15	7,011	8,542	7,944
20	9,855	13,122	11,890
25	13,852	20,276	17,902
30	19,469	31,455	27,058

money should accumulate in a variable annuity for at least fifteen years. If you cannot leave the money locked up for that long, do not buy a variable annuity.

• Variable annuities are best for taxpayers who will be in a lower tax bracket after the accumulation phase than during it. Taxpayers who anticipate being in the same bracket during both phases can benefit from a variable annuity if there is a long accumulation phase. Higher-income taxpayers who are concerned about the possibility of even higher tax rates in the future should carefully compare the variable annuity with other options.

• Performance counts. Variable annuities make sense only if the investments in it earn high returns. As a good rule of thumb, do not make low-return investments in a variable annuity or other deferral vehicle. The yield is too low to overcome the additional expenses and benefit from the deferral. Instead, stocks and other potential top returners should be allowed to compound in the deferred account.

• Relative performance counts. Remember that in a variable annuity you can invest only in the funds made available to you by the insurer. Too many people have purchased variable annuities that offer mediocre or below-average stock funds. The result is that they would have been better off investing in quality mutual funds in a taxable account. So you need to check out the performance of the funds or subaccounts offered with the annuity. Good sources of variable annuity subaccount performance data are *Barron's* and Morningstar. The best source probably is Morningstar.

• The higher the costs imposed by the annuity, the more the investment funds in the annuity have to outperform other options. The lowest-cost variable annuities are offered by mutual fund companies: Vanguard, Scudder, and Fidelity, in order from lowest to highest costs. The costs for the average variable annuity are about 2.12 percent of your account value each year. Before investing make sure you have identified *all* the costs that will be subtracted from your return.

• Look for flexibility and options. The low-cost annuities just mentioned offer only a few investment options. For slightly higher costs you can buy variable annuities that offer two dozen or more investment choices.

• You should be prepared to withdraw money from the variable annuity in increments instead of taking a lump sum after fifteen or twenty years of annuitizing the account. The longer you can use the tax deferral and earn high returns, the better it is for you. Avoid a policy with restrictions on how you can withdraw the cash.

• Be sure the insurer is financially sound. Check the ratings with the various rating services and invest only with the most secure insurance companies.

Variable Life Insurance

The latest insurance innovation, and another hot seller, is variable life or variable universal life insurance.

A big advantage that variable life supposedly has over variable annuities is that if the life policy meets some complicated tax law requirements, you can borrow from the policy's cash value—usually up to 90 percent of the value. The loans are nontaxable transactions. So, unlike a variable annuity, you can get access to your account value without paying taxes. Technically you do not have to repay the loans. At your death, the outstanding loans simply reduce the death benefit paid to your beneficiaries.

Because of the tax-free loan provision, variable life sometimes is promoted as an alternative to pension plans or as a college savings plan. But you have to look at the whole package of advantages and disadvantages, as well alternative investments, before deciding that variable life is appropriate.

The main difference between variable life and traditional whole life is the same as the difference between variable annuities and fixed annuities. Variable life lets you choose how your cash value account is invested from among the funds offered by the insurer. If you pick winning funds, the cash value and insurance benefit will increase much faster than under whole life. Earnings in the cash value account accumulate tax-deferred.

When considering a variable life proposal, there are some important points to keep in mind.

• As with variable annuities, variable life looks attractive only when a high rate of return is assumed. If you cannot expect at least a 10 percent average annual return from your investment choices, variable life probably is not for you.

• Many variable life proposals make extreme assumptions so that the policies compare favorably with other investment options.

• You pay for life insurance under variable life, and it is the most expensive way to buy life insurance. Compare the cost of insurance under the variable life policy with reasonably priced term insurance that you would buy if you were to invest through taxable mutual funds.

• Don't buy more life insurance than you need just to get the tax deferral on the cash value account. There are cheaper, more effective ways to build up cash.

• Be sure to check the provisions on withdrawals and loans and make sure that the illustration makes realistic assumptions about these.

• As with a variable annuity, the investment performance of the mutual funds offered with the policy matter a lot. Don't buy the policy if there is no history of above-average returns.

Loan traps. Under most variable life policies, when you take a loan against your cash value, that portion of the cash value no longer earns the return generated by the investments you selected. Instead, a fixed rate of interest is credited to your account until the loan is repaid. So once you start taking loans, you begin to lose the high returns.

In addition, you can borrow only up to 90 percent of the cash value. Be sure that under realistic assumptions you will be able to meet the future spending needs with 90 percent of the projected cash value.

A policy lapse could occur if you borrow too much money or the rate of return on your cash value falls. To prevent a lapse you have to pay additional premiums. If you let the policy lapse, any loans you have taken are immediately taxable to you.

Tax wise money strategy. Probably the best case for variable universal life insurance is that of a taxpayer who wants an investment fund that can be tapped in emergencies but mainly wants to leave a lot of money to children or other heirs or to pay estate taxes. With a variable life policy, the tax-free life insurance that would go to the beneficiaries normally would far exceed the premiums you paid, plus you would be able to take loans against the cash value if you have an emergency.

Before considering a variable life product as an investment vehicle, maximize your use of company retirement plans, 401(k)s, IRAs, and annuities.

The Private Pension Plan, Super Annuity

You might have heard of a special type of insurance product that is called a "private pension plan" or "super annuity."

Actually these products are plain, old whole life insurance that qualify as modified endowment contracts (MECs) under the tax law. But they get the other names because you are advised to use them as both savings vehicles and as life insurance.

A modified endowment contract is one that has a minimum amount of life insurance for each dollar of cash value. In addition, you generally must pay premiums into the policy for at least seven years. If a policy meets these and other technical requirements, you can borrow from the cash value tax-free.

Here is how some propose that you use an MEC today as a savings plan. A thirty-five-year-old can buy a $100,000 life insurance policy for premiums of a little over $1,000 annually. After twenty years the premiums have totaled more than $21,000, and the cash value is about $31,000. The policyholder then can borrow $25,000 of the cash value tax-free. The insurance company estimates that the remaining cash value will earn enough income to pay future premiums to keep the policy in force for about eleven years. After all the dust clears, the policyholder comes out $4,000 ahead and has had the insurance coverage for thirty-one years. Alternatively, a smaller amount of cash value could be borrowed each year.

The MEC could be used in this way to save for a college education, retirement, or as a supplement to your investment program.

But there are some pitfalls in this scheme.

One pitfall is that the insurance company does not guarantee the projected returns on your cash value. When returns are below the projections, the policy will lapse sooner than predicted, or the cash value will grow more slowly than projected. That means you get a lower benefit, or the insurance ends up costing more than anticipated.

In addition, when a policy lapses you must include all the outstanding policy loans in your income for the year of the lapse. So your options when the policy is about to lapse are to repay some or all of the loans, pay additional premiums, or pay taxes on money you already spent.

Another potential disadvantage is that the insurance benefits are included in your estate for tax purposes. Your heirs can receive the insurance benefits free of income taxes, but estate taxes will be due.

Tax wise money strategy: Consider these "private pension plans" only for excess money after you have exhausted all the other tax-deferral possibilities and have a substantial investment portfolio. The primary goal of the insurance should be either to pay for an expense that might arise on your premature death or to provide additional money for your heirs.

Taking Out Your Cash

Building up a nice balance in your annuity or life insurance policy is only half the battle. You want to withdraw the money in the most advantageous way for you. Only then will you have maximized after-tax wealth.

Unfortunately, many insurers offer good front-end deals and take the money away on the back end. To avoid getting burned when you can afford it least, consider your withdrawal strategy and options *before* buying the policy.

Withdrawal restrictions. You want maximum flexibility when it comes time to take money out of an annuity. Definitely avoid an annuity that *requires* you to "annuitize" through that policy. Annuitizing means you withdraw the account balance in fixed periodic payments, usually over your life or the joint lives of you and a beneficiary.

Many annuities pay one interest rate during the accumulation phase, then credit a much lower rate to your account balance during the payout phase. Sometimes the payout phase interest rate is so low that you are better off taking a lump-sum withdrawal, paying taxes, and investing the after-tax balance yourself. To determine if an annuity falls into that category, compare its "settlement rate" (the yield credited during the payout phase) to its crediting rate (the yield credited during the accumulation phase). Both figures should be defined in the policy. You also can compare the annuity's guaranteed payout per $1,000 of account value with the payout offered by current immediate annuity contracts.

Ideally, you want the full package of payout options: annuitizing that annuity, transferring the account balance to an immediate annuity with that company, making a tax-free exchange for an immediate annuity with another insurer, and taking a lump-sum withdrawal.

Increase Your Annuity Income by 20 Percent

Most retirees think that once they have decided to take an annuity instead of a lump sum, they should take the annuity payout offered by their current insurer or pension plan. This can be a very expensive mistake.

Annuity payouts depend on assumptions about your life expectancy, the assumed investment return on the account, and the expenses of administering the annuity and the account. These assumptions vary greatly among payers.

For example, there are several standard mortality tables that can be used to determine your life expectancy. The longer the assumed life expectancy, the lower the annual payout to you. Many insurers use their own mortality experience instead of standard mortality tables. Similarly, each pension fund and insurance company has its own investment experience and assumptions about future investment returns. Further, each payer charges different levels of expenses for administering the annuity, and these expenses reduce your payout. Even small differences in any or all of these assumptions can make a big difference in your annual payout. These differences multiplied by your life expectancy result in an enormous amount of money.

It is not unusual for the same person to be quoted widely different annuity payouts at the same time from different payers. The difference can be as much as 20 percent. That is 20 percent a month, every month, for the rest of your life.

Tax wise money strategy: To ensure that you are getting the highest, safe monthly income you can, get several quotes for annuity payouts. Then select the annuity that pays the highest amount and is offered by a safe, secure payer.

I did such a search for an individual whose pension plan was offering an annuity payout of $685 a month. Insurers with good safety ratings were offering the following payouts from immediate annuities that could be purchased with the lump-sum value of the individual's account:

Insurer 1	$703.33
Insurer 2	591.00
Insurer 3	657.40
Insurer 4	690.30
Insurer 5	717.20

That is a 20 percent difference between the highest and the lowest insurer, and all these insurers had good safety ratings. If you feel comfortable with insurers with lower credit ratings, you could get even higher quotes. (Annuity payouts change as interest rates change, so the numbers in this example do not reflect the payouts you could get today.)

Tax-free switch. Suppose you decide to annuitize your policy and decide that the best deal is an immediate annuity offered by another insurer. You can make a tax-free exchange of annuity contracts. You don't have to withdraw the money from your current annuity, pay taxes, and reinvest the after-tax cash in the new annuity. Instead, have your current account balance transferred directly to the new insurer. That qualifies as a tax-free exchange under Section 1034 of the tax code.

The IRS has ruled that the tax-free exchange of annuities applies to an exchange of a U.S. annuity for a Swiss annuity. So if you already have a number of U.S. annuities and want to diversify into foreign annuities, you should be able to do so with a tax-free exchange (Private Letter Ruling 9319024).

Chapter 8

The Return of Tax Shelters

The Tax Reform Act of 1986 went a long way toward eliminating tax shelters, but the Clinton tax code created some new tax shelters, enhanced others, and raised tax rates so that tax shelters became more attractive. Bill Clinton specifically stated after his election that he disagreed with the tax reform notion of eliminating tax shelters by lowering tax rates and reducing write-offs. Instead, he wanted the tax code to encourage certain types of investments by raising tax rates while giving investors tax breaks for spending or investing their money in certain ways.

A tax shelter is an investment that reduces income taxes in perfectly legal ways. In this chapter we'll explore the passive activity rules that tax reform used to limit tax shelters, the loopholes in those rules, and the investment tax shelters that are available today to help you build after-tax wealth.

The Disadvantages of Passive Activities

The passive activity rules were the centerpiece of the attack on tax shelters. Losses from a "passive activity" can be deducted only against income from passive activities. You cannot deduct a passive activity loss against salary, business income, or investment income. A passive activity loss that cannot be deducted this year is carried forward to future tax years until you have passive activity income against which the loss can be deducted. Or, in the year in which you dispose of a passive activity, the entire accumulated loss from the activity can be deducted against any type of income.

Under the passive activity rules there are three types of activities: portfolio, passive, and nonpassive.

A portfolio activity generates interest, dividends, annuities, gain or loss from property sales, and royalties that are not generated by your business activities.

A passive activity is any trade or business in which you do not materially participate, though you will learn about exceptions for working oil and gas interests and some real-estate activities.

A nonpassive activity is any trade or business that is not a passive or portfolio activity. Losses from this type of activity can be deducted against any type of income.

Tax wise money strategy. When you expect an activity to generate losses, you want to participate materially in the activity so you can deduct the losses against any type of income. But if you already have passive losses, you might want to structure any new income-generating activity as a passive one so the income will be sheltered by your passive losses.

Avoiding Passive Activities

One way to avoid the passive activity loss limitations is to materially participate in a business activity. There are seven tests to determine if your participation is material, but only two of the tests are useful to most taxpayers. The main test requires you to participate in the activity for more than five hundred hours during the tax year. The other useful test is the significant-participation test. A significant participation activity is one in which your total participation is *more than* one hundred hours. If your total hours in all your significant participation activities for the year are more than five hundred, then you are considered to materially participate in each of the significant participation activities.

Special situations. Rental activities automatically are passive activities unless the rental is short-term and significant services are provided along with the property that is rented (e.g., in hotels). So you might never be a material participant in a rental activity, regardless of the number of hours you put in. A limited partner generally is not a material participant unless the partner participated for more than five hundred hours during the year.

Audit alert. Auditors now carefully examine large or regular losses on tax returns. You can expect to have to prove that the activity is a business and not a hobby, that you materially participated in it, and that the expenses all are legitimate.

Passive Loss Loopholes

As with every part of the tax code, there are some useful loopholes in the passive loss rules. Many taxpayers can use one or more of these loopholes to advantage.

Corporate loophole. The passive activity rules apply to individuals, most trusts, estates, personal service corporations (those owned by professionals such as doctors and lawyers), and closely held regular corporations. A closely held corporation is one in which five or fewer individuals own more than 50 percent of the value of the outstanding stock. This means that many regular corporations still can benefit from old-fashioned tax shelters. For partnerships and S corporations, the passive loss rules are applied to each individual owner. So the income or loss might be passive to one owner and nonpassive to another owner.

Real-Estate Rentals

The passive activity restrictions also do not apply to real-estate rental losses of up to $25,000 for individuals with adjusted gross incomes under $100,000. For adjusted gross incomes between $100,000 and $150,000, the $25,000 loss allowance is phased out. Any unused portion of the $25,000 allowance is not carried forward to future years.

Caution. The $25,000 real-estate rental loss allowance is not available to married taxpayers who file separate returns.

To qualify for this exception you must own at least 10 percent and actively participate in the activity. Active participation means being part of management decisions or arranging for others to provide services. Management decisions include approving tenants, deciding on rental terms, approving capital expenditures or repairs, and similar decisions. You can have a management company run the property for you as long as your agreement with the management company spells out the rental terms and gives you final approval over tenants, repairs, and improvements.

Old-Fashioned Real-Estate Write-Offs

Under the 1993 tax hike, real-estate professionals can deduct passive real-estate rental losses against other types of income in the year the losses are incurred—just as in the days before tax reform.

To qualify as a real-estate professional, more than 50 percent of your personal services for the year must be performed in a real-estate trade or business, and you must perform more than 750 hours of personal services in a real-estate business in which you materially participate. Work done as an employee does not count unless you own 5 percent or more of the business. A closely held corporation qualifies as being in real estate if more than 50 percent of its gross receipts were derived from a real-estate trade or business.

Unfortunately, this write-off applies only to new real-estate losses, not to those incurred and suspended before the effective date of the new rules, December 31, 1993.

Tax wise money strategy. Perhaps the biggest loophole this creates is for married couples filing joint returns. If one spouse qualifies as being in a real-estate trade or business, all real-estate rental investment losses of the couple can be deducted on their joint return.

Oil and Gas Investments

Some oil and gas investments completely avoid the passive activity loss rules and offer unlimited tax write-offs.

To get the unlimited tax write-offs you must assume unlimited personal liability for the debts and obligations of the investment. In addition, the investment must be a "working interest" in an oil and gas property that is burdened with the costs of drilling, development, or operation of the property. A simple royalty interest or production payment does not qualify.

Fortunately, the "unlimited" personal liability can be limited. Liability insurance can be purchased by the investment sponsor to give you a large cushion. In addition, the IRS has ruled that you can keep your deductions if, after taking the initial drilling deductions, your general partnership interest is converted to a limited partnership interest.

Deductions from oil and gas drilling investments can be substantial. Investors generally are allowed an immediate write-off for the costs, known as intangible drilling costs, instead of writing off the start-up costs over a period of years, as with most investments. The first-year deduction can be 50 percent to 90 percent of your investment.

Once the oil or gas starts to flow, there is another tax break, known as the depletion allowance. The idea is that the natural resource you paid for is being depleted, so you ought to get a write-off against the income, just as a real-estate or equipment owner gets a depreciation write-off.

Tax wise money strategy. The tax breaks aren't enough to justify this investment unless the project produces oil or gas for a number of years. You really need someone who is familiar with the oil and gas industry to tell you if the investment is likely to be economically viable.

AMT alert. While these oil and gas investments avoid the passive activity rules, they do not avoid the alternative minimum tax. You could end up with substantially reduced tax benefits if you put a lot of money in oil and gas deals without checking the potential AMT effects first.

Low-Income Housing

Another traditional tax shelter that survived tax reform is the tax credit for investments in low-income housing. Under the current rules, you could get an annual tax credit of $9,900 each year for ten years, or a total of $99,000 over ten years—even if you are a passive investor.

Low-income housing investments are fairly straightforward. You put cash into low-income housing projects, usually through a limited partnership. Each year for the next ten years you get a tax credit that directly reduces your tax bill.

The amount of the credit depends on the type of low-income housing that is purchased or built. In addition, the IRS issues tables each month that adjust the amount of the credit for changes in interest rates. Most of the time the highest credit is 8 percent to 9 percent of your initial investment. So if you invest $50,000, you could get a tax credit of $4,000 to $4,500 each year for the next ten years.

Most low-income housing partnerships use a moderate amount of debt to finance their properties. This can increase your tax credits on average to about 15 percent of your investment, or 150 percent of your investment over ten years.

A tax credit is more valuable than a deduction of the same amount. A tax credit is subtracted directly from your tax due for the year. A dollar of credit eliminates a dollar of taxes. But a deduction is subtracted from your income; then the tax rate is applied to the remaining income. In the 36 percent tax bracket, a dollar of deductions reduces your tax bill by 36 cents.

Some low-income housing projects give a double benefit. They invest in low-income housing in rural areas and qualify for special low-interest rate financing from the Farmers' Home Administration. This helps the project generate positive cash flow for investors.

Tax credit limits. The tax credit is limited to the equivalent of a $25,000 deduction. To determine your limit, multiply your marginal tax bracket by $25,000. If you are in the 39.6 percent tax bracket, your maximum annual credit is $9,900. In addition, you cannot use the full tax credit if you also are using the $25,000 real-estate rental-loss allowance.

Avoiding the Pitfalls

To get the tax credits, the partnership must own the property for at least fifteen years. You will not be able to get your principal back before then, and probably longer. In addition, you never know if the housing can be sold in the future or what the price will be. In your planning, you should not count on a capital gain from the sale. Cash flow from most low-income housing projects tends to be low or even nonexistent. Do not count on cash distributions, either, when considering the investment.

Low-income housing also has the usual problems of partnership investments. There are fees on the front end that are subtracted from your investment before determining the amount of your tax credit. The investment is illiquid and must be held for a long time. As with most partnerships, the individual investor is at the general partner's mercy on all actions.

AMT alert. If you are subject to the alternative minimum tax, the low-income housing tax credit is of no use to you. The credit cannot be used when computing tax under the AMT.

Tax wise money strategy. An 8 percent to 15 percent rate of return is not good enough for most taxpayers, given the risks, lack of liquidity, and inflexibility of this investment. But if you have substantial assets so that the liquidity is not a problem and you are confident of avoiding the minimum tax, look at low-income housing.

Rehabilitating Buildings

Another tax credit is available for expenses incurred to rehabilitate old buildings. The credit is equal to 20 percent of the qualified rehabilitation expenditures incurred on a certified historic structure, or 10 percent of the qualified rehabilitation expenditures on a building that was first placed in service before 1936.

The rehabilitation credit is exempt from the passive activity rules until the investor's adjusted gross income exceeds $200,000. Then the credit is reduced by 50 percent of the amount by which your AGI exceeds $200,000. You also are allowed to take depreciation deductions on the amount of the building's cost that exceeds the rehabilitation credit, but depreciation and other deductions are subject to the passive-loss rules.

The certified historic structure credit is available for both residential and nonresidential buildings. But the credit for noncertified buildings is available only for nonresidential buildings.

Sheltering Stock Profits

The Clinton tax code created two capital gains breaks for investors in certain small businesses.

Deferring Capital Gains

The first break allows you to defer capital gains from the sale of publicly traded stocks and bonds if the sale proceeds are invested in the stock of a specialized small business investment company (SSBIC) within sixty days of the sale. An SSBIC is a firm that invests in businesses owned by minority or disadvantaged individuals and is certified as such by the Small Business Administration. There is an annual limit of $50,000 on the amount of gain that may be rolled over in this way.

Example. You own $100,000 of stocks that have a capital gain of $50,000. If you sell the stocks, your capital gains tax will be $14,250. You can defer this tax by investing the entire $100,000 sale proceeds in the stocks of an SSBIC.

Tax wise money strategy. This tax shelter is only for money you can afford to lose and will not need access to for many years. You are taking money out of a liquid, publicly traded investment and putting it in an illiquid investment. A nonpublic small business also is one of the riskier investments you can make. The deferral strategy is useless if your reason for selling the publicly traded securities was to raise cash.

Exempting Capital Gains

The second capital gains tax break is for investments in certain small business stock. If you buy small business stock and hold the stock for at least five years, when the stock is sold, 50 percent of the capital gain is excluded from gross income. This break applies to stock purchased through partnerships as well as stock purchased directly. Investment bankers already are putting together partnerships to exploit this credit.

There are several disadvantages to this investment.

First, many types of businesses do not qualify. In fact, after reviewing the extensive list of businesses that are excluded, it seems that only a manufacturing or technology firm will meet the definition of a qualified trade or business.

Second, this will be an illiquid investment. To qualify as a small business, the business cannot have more than $50 million in assets. So it either will not be publicly traded or will be very thinly traded.

Third, since this is a small business investment, it is risky.

AMT alert. While 50 percent of the gain on the stock can be excluded from income under the regular income tax, that is not the case under the alternative minimum tax. Half of the excluded gain is a preference item for the AMT, and of course half of the total gain is included in income anyway. So the overall tax on your capital gain probably will be about 24 percent, a savings of only 4 percentage points below the regular capital gains tax rate of 28 percent. That is not much of an incentive to invest in an illiquid, risky enterprise.

More Oil and Gas Benefits

You can get tax benefits from an oil and gas deal without the unlimited risk of a working interest discussed earlier. You won't get the big first-year deduction, because you will not avoid the passive activity rules. But your income from the investment will be partially sheltered by the percentage depletion allowance and further sheltered by the deduction for intangible drilling costs.

Tax wise money strategy: Investors who already have substantial, diversified portfolios should consider oil and gas investments as an additional diversification. You should get inflation protection since this is a natural resource investment, and a good program will produce tax-sheltered high yields.

Enter the Corporate Leasing World

Equipment leasing still provides tax benefits, though not the great benefits before tax reform. A good equipment leasing program generates a fairly high cash yield after paying all expenses. This yield is partly sheltered by interest and depreciation deductions. If you have suspended passive activity losses from other investments, those losses can shelter the net income from the equipment leasing deal.

Tax wise money strategy. The main problems with equipment leasing deals in the past have been economic. Too often, the equipment is obsolete before the useful life is over, so the lessee returns the equipment and leases something else. Or the lessee experiences financial problems and cannot make lease payments. At other times, too many partnerships are formed to lease a particular type of equipment, and the glut forces leasing prices down. In all these cases, investors have to pay debt on equipment that is essentially worthless. In a leasing deal, you need to examine the basic business prospects before even looking at potential tax benefits.

An investment must have more than tax benefits to make it worthwhile. You must consider all the financial risks, the cash flow, potential appreciation, liquidity, flexibility, amount of capital required, and the diversification of your portfolio. If an investment would make no sense at all without the tax benefits, it probably is not a good idea unless the tax benefits are exceptional and you do not take on debt to make the investment.

Chapter 9

Charitable Giving as a Top Tax Shelter

One activity Congress continues to encourage through tax advantages is charitable giving. In addition to providing tax benefits, a number of charitable giving strategies, many of them little known, can help you solve retirement, financial, and estate planning problems. With a well-designed gift you could end up in a better financial situation than you were in before the gift—while helping out the charity.

High-income alert. Charitable contribution deductions are subject to the itemized deduction reduction described in Chapter 13. If your adjusted gross income is going to exceed $111,800 this year, be sure to factor the itemized deduction reduction into any charitable contribution tax planning you do.

Itemizers only. You get a tax benefit from charitable contributions only if your total itemized deductions exceed the standard deduction.

Basic Contribution Rules

The basic charitable contribution is a modest donation by cash or check. You can deduct these contributions as long as the charity is one that qualifies under Section 501(c)(3) of the tax code.

These nonproperty charitable contribution deductions are limited to 50 percent of your adjusted gross income when the contributions are made to public charities, educational institutions, religious organizations, and a few other types of charities. Contributions to some other types of charities are limited to 30 percent of adjusted gross income. Excess contributions can be carried forward and deducted on future tax returns for up to five years.

Beware of quid pro quo. Many charities promise a gift, known as a premium, in return for a contribution. The IRS and Congress decided that if you are receiving a gift in return for your contribution, you are not really making the contribution in the spirit of generosity that justifies a full charitable contribution deduction. Your deduction is reduced by the value of the premium. When a contribution exceeds $75, a charity needs to inform you of the value of any premium you receive, and only the contribution amount that exceeds the value of the goods or services furnished is deductible.

Written receipt required. In the 1993 tax hike, Congress required that beginning in 1994 you need to have a written receipt or acknowledgment to deduct charitable contributions of $250 or more. The acknowledgment must be received by the earlier of the date you file the return and the due date for the return, including extensions. The receipt must state the amount of the cash contributed and a description, but not the value, of any property donated, along with a description and good-faith estimate of the value of any goods or services you received in return for the contribution.

Tax wise money strategy. The IRS does not give the charities a deadline for issuing their acknowledgments. It is up to you to find out when the charity plans to issue written acknowledgments and to follow up well before your tax return is due to ensure that you have the acknowledgments in hand.

Tax wise money strategy. One way to give a substantial amount to a charity without worrying about acknowledgments is through a payroll deduction plan at work. IRS regulations say the written receipt requirement applies only to deductions on an individual paycheck that are $250 or more. You need a written record from the employer showing the amount deducted from your salary and contributed to charity.

Audit alert. Contributions for which a written acknowledgment is not required still must be documented by a contemporaneous written record to be deductible. Canceled checks or receipts are the best records but are not required. An alternative is a written log of your charitable contributions. Update it regularly throughout the year; this should be a sufficient written record to support a charitable contribution deduction.

Contributions of Services

You might volunteer your time instead of or in addition to giving money. The value of your time or services does not qualify for a charitable contribution deduction, even if you are in the business of providing the service that you gave to the charity.

But out-of-pocket expenses you incur while doing charitable volunteer work are deductible. When using your car for charitable activities, you can take a standard mileage deduction of 12 cents for each mile driven, if the mileage is not reimbursed. You also can deduct parking fees and tolls. Instead of using the standard mileage allowance, you can use the actual expense method to determine your charitable deduction for using your automobile, but you cannot deduct a portion of general repair or maintenance, depreciation, insurance, registration fees, and similar expenses.

Travel expenses, including meals and lodging while out of town, are deductible when incurred while performing services for charity if there is not a significant element of personal benefit or pleasure in the trip. Any meal expenses incurred while traveling out of town for charitable work must be reduced by 50% before taking the deduction.

You also can deduct the cost of supplies and equipment you need to perform charitable services. For example, Scout leaders generally can deduct the cost of uniforms. Materials and supplies that you purchase and donate to the group also are deductible.

Tax wise money strategy. Keep track of the expenses you incur while performing charitable activities, including automobile mileage. People who are active in Scout groups and civic organizations often throw away hundreds of dollars of charitable contribution deductions each year by not keeping records of their mileage and out-of-pocket expenses.

Contributions of Property

You don't have to give cash to a charity to get a charitable deduction. You can be like the Clintons and give away your old underwear and socks. Or you can donate furniture, cars, stocks, bonds, books, collectibles, art, jewelry, real estate, coin collections, or virtually any other type of property you might own.

When you give appreciated capital gain property that you have held for more than twelve months, the fair market value is deductible. Capital gain property basically is any property other than business inventory. In addition, the gift is not treated as a sale, so you do not recognize gain or loss.

Tax wise money strategy. Do not donate property in which you have a paper loss. You will not get to use the loss and will deduct only the current fair market value of the property. The charity, since it is tax-exempt, gets no tax benefit from the loss either. A better strategy is to sell the property, take your tax loss, and donate the cash proceeds from the sale to the charity. That gives you a double deduction: the loss and the charitable contribution.

Deductions of appreciated property contributions are limited to 30 percent of adjusted gross income, instead of the 50 percent limit than applies to most cash contributions. You can get the 50 percent limit on the property contributions if you elect to reduce the fair market value of the property by the amount of the appreciation that would have been long-term capital gains if the property had been sold.

Caution. If you donate tangible personal property and the charity does not use the property in its exempt function, your deduction is limited to your basis in the property.

Tax wise money strategy. When giving tangible capital gain property (art, books, collections) to a charity, have the charity agree in writing that it will use the property solely in its exempt functions. Also, be sure to donate property only to organizations that can use it properly. Donate art to a museum, not to a hospital.

Inventory

If you donate inventory or other "ordinary income property" to a charity, the deduction is your tax basis in the property. Corporations and S corporations that donate inventory held for resale to retail customers may also deduct up to half of the appreciation, provided the deduction does not exceed twice the donor's basis in the property. The donation must be used for the care of the ill, needy, or for infants, and cannot be transferred by the charity for money. To get the deduction, the donor must receive a written statement from the charity that it will comply with these requirements.

Reporting Property Contributions

When a noncash contribution exceeds $500, you must attach Form 8283 to your return. (Regular corporations that are not personal service corporations or closely held corporations file Form 8283 when noncash contributions exceed $5,000.) This form asks for a description of the property, the date you purchased it, and the purchase price.

When a noncash contribution exceeds $5,000, you also need a receipt or other acknowledgment from the charity, and a qualified appraisal of the property. An appraisal is not required for donations of publicly traded securities and for some donations of nonpublicly traded securities. The regulations set out specific requirements of the appraisal.

Audit alert. The IRS aggressively challenges the values of many charitable contributions of property. The IRS even maintains its own board of outside art valuation experts, who have been key to getting many charitable contribution deductions reduced.

Special Charitable Giving Strategies

You can use the basic charitable deduction rules to devise creative charitable giving strategies that combine tax benefits with other financial benefits.

Avoiding Capital Gains Taxes

Suppose you have $100,000 worth of mutual funds that cost you $50,000. You have a $50,000 capital gain, which means taxes of $14,000 and net proceeds of only $86,000 if you sell them.

Tax wise money strategy. Consider donating the mutual funds to charity instead of selling them. You get a charitable contribution deduction of $100,000 if you held the funds for more than one year (subject to the annual deduction limit). If that exceeds your contribution limit of 50 percent of adjusted gross income, you can carry the excess forward to your next five tax years. Your contribution to charity avoids capital gains taxes and uses the fair market value of the funds to reduce your taxes substantially. This strategy is especially useful if you were going to sell the stocks and make a substantial contribution to charity anyway—either this year or over the next few years.

Avoid Capital Gains Taxes, Keep Income

Suppose you want to make a charitable contribution, but you need income from the property to maintain your standard of living. In that case, consider the charitable remainder trust. This trust gives you triple tax benefits: you avoid capital gains taxes, get a current deduction, and avoid estate taxes on the property. In addition, you get lifetime income from the property. Details of this strategy are in the chapter on avoiding capital gains taxes.

Pension Fund Substitute

The charitable remainder trust also can be a supplemental pension fund. Many upper-income employees and business owners are looking for pension fund substitutes, since qualified pension plan benefits were reduced under the last few tax laws. You can set up a charitable remainder trust and make contributions to it each year. You get to deduct part of each contribution. The trust invests the money, and the income and gains accumulate and compound tax-free. You can be trustee and invest the money the way you want. The trust has to be written carefully and the money properly invested so that income payouts are not required until your retirement. Then you can shift the portfolio and begin paying retirement income.

Protect Your Retirement Plan

Retirement plans are automatically included in your estate, and the main way to avoid estate taxes on them is to take the marital deduction by leaving the entire plan to your spouse. But an IRS ruling shows how to use a charitable trust to protect your pension from estate taxes, provide for your spouse, and provide for a charity.

In the ruling, the taxpayer had a substantial 401(k) plan. He set up a charitable remainder trust and named this as beneficiary of the plan. After the taxpayer's death, the entire plan assets were distributed to the trust. The distribution was tax-exempt, since the trust is charitable. If a distribution had been made to an individual or a taxable trust, the entire distribution would have been subject to income taxes. The trust will pay income to the spouse for the rest of her life. After her death, the balance of the trust goes to a charity. According to the IRS, the entire value of the 401(k) is included in the taxpayer's estate, but the value of the part that goes to the charity qualifies for the charitable deduction, and the rest qualifies for the marital deduction. So there is no estate tax on the plan, the spouse is provided for, and the charity will get a contribution. In addition, the spouse pays taxes on the income only as it is received (Letter Ruling 9253038).

Keep the Property, Give Away the Income

A charitable lead trust is the mirror image of a charitable remainder trust. You put property in a trust, and the trust pays income to the charity for a period of years designated by you. After that period ends, the property in the trust either is returned to you or goes to your children or other beneficiaries designated by you.

The advantages of this trust are that you get a current charitable deduction of the present value of the income and keep the property in your estate or family. The income paid to the charity is off your tax return, which is beneficial when you are in a high tax bracket. If the property goes to your children after the trust expires, then there would be a gift tax, but this gift tax would be less than if you had simply given the entire property to the children.

Give Away Part of Your Home

One way to tap your home equity is to give a charity a remainder interest in your home. You get a tax deduction today and still live in the house for the rest of your life. The amount of your tax deduction depends on your age, the value of the home, and current interest rates. The older you are, the larger the percentage of your home's value you can deduct.

Tax wise money strategy. Giving a remainder interest to charity works for many types of property, such as a farm or vacation home. In one case, a taxpayer kept art in his home but gave the charity a remainder interest, so that when he died the art would go to the charity. This gave him a tax deduction today for a donation of his art that would physically occur in the future, and he got to enjoy and display the art of for the rest of his life.

Collect an Annuity from Charity

A charitable gift annuity should be considered by charitably minded people who are saving for retirement.

Under the gift annuity, you give money to a charity in a lump sum or installments. These payments are part charitable contribution, and you get a deduction for that part. The rest of the payments purchase an annuity— a promise of a future stream of payments from the charity. When you receive the annuity payments, part of each payment is a tax-free return of principal, and part is interest income.

You will pay more for the charitable gift annuity than you would for an annuity issued by a for-profit insurance company that makes the same payments to you. The difference between the income from the charitable annuity and from the for-profit annuity is your gift to the charity. The value of your charitable contribution deduction is determined from tables issued by the IRS. Most major charities have charitable gift annuity programs in place; you should be able to learn the annuity payments you would receive by asking the charity's planned giving office.

Give Away Life Insurance

A quick and easy way for many people to boost charitable contribution deductions is to transfer to a charity ownership of a cash value life insurance policy you don't need. The transfer gives you an immediate charitable contribution deduction. Valuing the deduction is a little tricky, and you probably should have a tax expert determine the deduction amount for you. But you generally deduct the amount of the cash value at the time you make the transfer. If you continue to make future premium payments on the policy, a portion of those payments will be deductible.

Giving away a life insurance policy also provides benefits to the charity. The charity can cash in the policy, borrow from the cash value, or wait to collect the death benefit.

Give Away Air or Development Rights

Real-estate owners can generate an easy tax deduction by granting a charity certain rights known as an easement. There are several types of easements that qualify for deductions.

An **open space easement** means that you and future owners cannot undertake certain types of development on the property. The easement gives the charity you designate (including a government) the right to enforce the easement. The easement might restrict the number, type, and height of buildings, removal of trees, removal of structures, placement of utility lines, dumping of trash, and use of signs, to give a few common examples.

A **conservation easement** prevents certain types of use of the property. The law allows deductions for conservation easements that achieve objectives such as the preservation of land for outdoor recreation or education of the public, protection of a relativley natural habitat, preservation of farmland, forestland, or other open spaces, or preservation of historically important land or a certified historic structure. Taxpayers have taken conservation easement deductions by contributing the air space above their buildings or their building facades to charities.

Once an easement is given, it cannot be taken back. The easement will permanently reduce the value of the property you retain and also your flexibility in using the property. It could make the property difficult to sell.

Give Your Corporate Stock

Corporate owners might be able to deduct contributions that are effectively made by their corporations. The strategy is known as the charitable stock bailout.

Example. You are sole owner of a corporation valued at $5 million. You give corporate stock valued at $100,000 to a charity. Because this is appreciated capital gain property, you take a charitable deduction for the fair market value of the stock. After a period of time has passed, the corporation redeems the stock from the charity, paying cash for the stock.

This transaction works as long as the charity is not legally bound to have the stock redeemed by the corporation. The charity must be able to remain a shareholder of the corporation if it wants to.

Bargain Sales to Charity

You might have a piece of appreciated property that you can give to charity. The problem is that the property is worth more than you want to contribute, and there is no reasonable way to give only a portion of the property.

Tax wise money strategy. Make a bargain sale of the property to the charity. The charity gives you cash, but less cash than the property is worth. On your tax return you report this transaction partly as a sale of property and partly as a charitable contribution.

Give Away the Right to Use Property

A taxpayer owned a valuable art collection. He gave a museum part ownership of the art, allowing the museum to display the art for a certain number of days each year. On a sale of the art, the taxpayer and museum would split the proceeds proportionately. The taxpayer was allowed a deduction for the pro rata value of the art that he gave to the charity, though the museum never chose to display the art (*Winokur,* 90 TC 733).

Tax wise money strategy. This strategy works for different types of property. If you own a vacation home, you can donate a partial ownership that gives the charity the right to use the property during off-season periods when you wouldn't use it or rent it. The charity can use the home for retreats, seminars, etc.

Create a Private Foundation

You can choose the charitable giving route of the Rockefellers, Fords, and of many professional athletes and entertainers. You establish a private foundation, give money to the foundation, and deduct your contribution. As the person who created the foundation, wrote its by-laws, and probably appointed its initial directors, you have a lot of control over how the money is disbursed. In addition, you and your family members can receive salaries as employees or board members if the payments are reasonable for the work done.

To prevent abuses, Congress and the IRS have established a number of rules and restrictions on private foundations. You get a lower limit on your deductions, and there are restrictions on how the foundation money can be used. Private foundations also must disburse a minimum percentage of their assets each year. If you can afford the legal fees to make sure you comply with the rules, the private foundation is a good way to get charitable contribution deductions while establishing a legacy and retaining some control over how the money is used.

Pool Contributions with Others

The tax law allows deductions for contributions to "pooled income funds," basically mutual funds established by public charities. A pooled income fund makes distributions to the donors that basically are pro rata shares of interest, dividends, and capital gains. When a donor dies, the charity receives the value of that donor's pro rata interest in the fund. You receive a deduction at the time you contribute money to the pooled fund, based on a formula using the highest rate of return earned by the fund in the previous three years.

The pooled income fund allows you to convert appreciated assets into income-producing assets without having to go through the trouble of setting up a charitable trust or foundation. You also do not have to worry about managing the money or finding a manager for the money. The disadvantage of the pooled income fund is that you lose flexibility and control over how the fund is structured and how the money is invested.

Keep It Local

Many localities have versions of pooled income funds and private foundations known as community foundations. All contributions are used locally. A possible advantage is that the contributions all are used locally. The foundation might limit its use of funds to certain types of activities in the community, or it might have a great deal of freedom in deciding which activities in the community can receive contributions.

Most community foundations allow four types of gifts. Unrestricted funds are put into a general account, and the board of directors decides how the money will be disbursed. For a field-of-interest gift, you designate the area you want to benefit: parks, schools, cancer research, etc. You have even more control over donor-advised funds. This category allows you to recommend potential charities to the board of directors. The board is not bound by your recommendations but usually gives great weight to them. You have the most control over donor-designated funds. These allow you to specify the charities or projects that will receive the contribution.

There are about four hundred community foundations in the United States, with assets estimated at more than $8 billion. You can get information about community foundations from the Council on Foundations, 202-467-0404.

Estate-Planning Strategies

Most of the strategies discussed here can be set up either during your life or in your will. You get an income-tax deduction if you make a charitable contribution during your lifetime. If the charitable gift is made under your will, the estate gets a charitable-contribution deduction. So charitable gifts in your will reduce estate taxes and can be structured to provide income or other financial benefits to your survivors.

Tax wise money strategy. There are many ways to do good while cutting your taxes. If you are interested in giving to a major charity, discuss your options with someone in the charity's planned giving office.

You can state your needs and goals, and the charity will explain which of the strategies in this chapter are available and appropriate. Or you can meet with a tax expert or estate planner who keeps up with the details of creative charitable giving.

Chapter 10

Retirement Planning for Late Starters: Building a Retirement Fund in a Hurry

Meet Max Profits and his wife, Rosie.

The Profits have almost put their kids through college, the house will soon be paid off, and they are looking toward retirement. But after a serious review of their finances situation, Max is worried.

Ideally you should start planning and saving for retirement at age forty or so. When Max and Rosie were forty, like most American families they were struggling to pay the mortgage and daily expenses while saving some money for college tuition. Also, Max and Rosie did not use the tax code to make them rich during those years.

But with those major lifetime expenses behind them, Max and Rosie are thinking seriously about paying for their retirement years and are looking for ways to make up for lost time. Their probable sources of retirement income are Social Security, IRAs to which they made a few contributions over the years, and a modest retirement plan from Max's employer. Right now the Profits will not have the money to enjoy the kind of retirement they want.

Fortunately, there are a number of special, tax-advantaged ways in which Max and Rosie's retirement fund can grow faster than it ever could without the help of the tax code.

Beginning the Retirement Fund

Let's look at the many tools that Max and Rosie found to accelerate the growth of their retirement fund. You might not be able to use all these tools, but the tools for which you can qualify will put you on the road to the kind of retirement you want and deserve.

The 401(k)

Max's first step was to go to his employer's benefits office and discuss the options regarding his 401(k) plan. In a 401(k) plan (also known as a salary deferral plan or cash or deferred arrangement), an employee elects to have a portion of his salary paid into a 401(k) account instead of included in his paycheck. No income taxes are due on the deferred salary, though Social Security and Medicare taxes are. You could defer no more than $9,240 in 1994, and the limit is indexed for inflation each year.

Another limit, known as the top-heavy rules, is designed to prevent highly compensated employees from getting a disproportionate benefit from 401(k) plans. If lower-salary employees do not participate in the 401(k) plan, the maximum contribution that upper-income employees can make is reduced. In addition, beginning in 1994 only the first $150,000 of compensation can be used to compute retirement plan benefits and contributions. Unfortunately, these two provisions sometimes limit the benefits available to middle-income employees such as Max.

An employer can put additional restrictions on your deferral. Some employers, for example, let you defer a maximum of 6 percent of salary.

The benefits office tells Max that for every dollar he defers, the employer will add 50 cents to his account. The employer contribution is not taxed to Max until he withdraws it from the account. This gives Max a 50 percent return on his money before considering any investment return. Some employers will make a higher matching contribution, some a lower amount or nothing at all.

Sometimes the matching contribution depends on your investment choice. If your account is invested in stock of the employer, your contribution might be matched dollar for dollar. But if you allocate your account to other investments, the employer's matching contribution might be less. The combination of Max's deferral and his employer's matching contribution cannot exceed $30,000 or 25 percent of salary, whichever is less.

The income earned by the money in Max's account compounds tax-deferred until Max withdraws it.

The Power of a 401(k)

You get more benefit from a 401(k) than from some other tax-deferral strategies, such as insurance products, because the additional costs are lower or nonexistent.

Suppose a 401(k) account earns 8 percent before taxes, salary increases are 4 percent annually, and each employee makes annual contributions until age sixty-two. Also, the employer contributes 50 cents for every dollar the employee defers, up to 6 percent of salary. Here are the account balances of some different employees at age sixty-five (remember, the employees still must pay taxes on the money when it is withdrawn):

Employees and Earnings	6% Annual Contribution	10% Annual Contribution
25-year-old earning $25,000	$797,788	$1,152,650
35-year-old earning $40,000	506,556	731,692
42-year-old earning $70,000	433,923	626,777
53-year-old earning $80,000	122,163	176,457

Investing the Account

Max also learns that he can decide how his 401(k) account is invested. Some employers or plan administrators decide how the accounts are invested. But more and more employers are letting employees select from at least three investment options: stocks, bonds, and a money market-type fund. Max's employer set up its 401(k) plan through a mutual fund company that allows Max to choose from ten different investment funds. Max can change the allocation every quarter.

Until now, the small amount that Max has contributed to the 401(k) account has been in a safe, guaranteed-return account. Most 401(k) money is invested in this type of account, and that is not a good thing. Retirement money should be invested for the long term, and the best long-term returns traditionally come from stocks. Max realizes he probably can get a higher return in the long term by increasing the investment allocation of stocks and ignoring short-term swings in the account's value. Because Max now is a long-term investor, he can ride out the temporary downswings and earn a higher long-term return than he would from the guaranteed-return account.

Tax wise money strategy. Max leaves the benefits office determined to defer the maximum amount of salary that his employer and the tax law allow. He realizes that he and Rosie could reduce or eliminate many expenditures without any effect on their comfort. In addition, he decides to invest the account primarily in stock funds.

401(k) Summary

The 401(k) is a *deferral tax shelter.* There are multiple deferral benefits that Max will gain from his 401(k) plan:

- deferral of income taxes on the salary contributed to the 401(k) account;
- deferral of income taxes on the employer's matching contribution;
- deferral of income taxes on earnings of the account.

When Max withdraws money from the 401(k) account, he can roll over the account to an IRA, withdraw the 401(k) in a lump sum, and elect to report the income under one of the favored averaging formulas, or turn the account into an insurance annuity and get guaranteed payments for life from his account.

401(k)s for Small-Business Owners

The 401(k) plan can be tailored to the needs of a small business and its owners. A simple example is a small business with two owner-employees and no other employees. Each owner takes home $200,000 annually. One owner is younger and has children. He wants to take all his salary in cash to meet current expenses. The other owner is older, has paid for the house and college, and wants to start salting away about $30,000 a year for retirement.

The company can set up a 401(k) plan under which the employer contributes $3 for each dollar an employee contributes. The older owner can elect to defer $7,500 of salary. This could be matched by a $22,500 contribution from the employer, leaving a total contribution of $30,000 in the account. The younger owner would elect to contribute nothing and would continue taking home all his salary.

If the business had several employees, this arrangement still would be possible. The cost of the matching contributions could be kept down by providing that the employer will provide the three-for-one matching for salary deferrals only up to a certain percentage of salary. The older executive's deferral of $7,500, for example, is only 3.75 percent of salary.

Hardship Withdrawal

The biggest argument that people make against putting money into a plan is that withdrawls from a 401(k) before retirement generally are prohibited. But the hardship withdrawal rules let you withdraw your money early if you have a "financial hardship" such as medical expenses, tuition, or the likelihood of losing your home. Check with your plan sponsor for specific rules for your plan.

If you qualify for a hardship withdrawal, you still owe income taxes on the distribution and probably also owe the 10 percent early withdrawal penalty tax if you are under age 59½. In addition, the employer must withhold 20 percent of the distribution for income taxes. Before taking a distribution under the hardship withdrawal rules, however, consider taking a loan from your 401(k) account if your plan permits loans.

The Super 401(k)

Max is feeling good about his decisions on the 401(k) plan. But he knows the 401(k) by itself will not be enough.

Max talks to his boss and discovers that his supervisor struck a deal with the employer known as a super 401(k), wraparound 401(k), or non-qualified 401(k).

These plans are a form of nonqualified retirement plan. A qualified retirement plan is one that meets all the requirements and restrictions for tax exemption in the tax code. For example, in a qualified 401(k) there are limits on the amount of salary each employee can defer, on the deferrals of upper-income employees, and there are requirements and restrictions on the employer's actions.

A nonqualified retirement plan has few of these restrictions. The employer decides how few or how many employees participate. There are no limits on the amount of salary that can be deferred or matched, except those established by the employer. And the employer and the employee decide the basic structure of the plan and how it is administered.

The key to a nonqualified 401(k) is to ensure that the employee is able to defer taxes on contributions. The IRS says that the employee is not taxed as long as the money is not received by or made available to the employee and there is a substantial risk that the employee might have to forfeit the money.

There have been many IRS rulings on this over the years. What they boil down to is that the employee defers the income as long as the employer remains the owner of any funds, insurance policy, or trust that funds the agreement, and if the employer were to declare bankruptcy and be liquidated, the employee would be only a general creditor of the employer and therefore might not be paid some or all of the deferred compensation. Obviously you do not want to enter into a nonqualified deferred compensation plan if you have concerns about the financial viability of the employer.

Under some deferred-compensation plans the employee might forfeit the money if he or she leaves the employer within a certain number of years. This provision is known as "golden handcuffs" and is done to ensure that valued employees stay with the employer.

The employer pays the real cost of nonqualified deferred compensation. The employer gets no deduction until the employee recognizes income.

Max decides that he can afford to defer more of his income without cutting into his current lifestyle. So he sets up an appointment to discuss including him in the super 401(k).

SERPs, Top Hats, and Rabbi Trusts

Every year Max usually gets a bonus and a salary increase. Max is an experienced, valuable employee and expects to continue receiving bonuses and pay increases. Max and Rosie conclude that they do not need additional current income. They can maintain their lifestyle on Max's salary minus the 401(k) deferrals. What they want to do is find more tax-advantaged ways to accumulate a retirement fund.

The principles of the nonqualified 401(k) plan also can be applied to future bonuses and raises to set up a nonqualified deferred compensation plan. The employee gets deferral of the compensation until it is received or made available, as long as there is a substantial risk of forfeiture through the employer's bankruptcy or other means.

Nonqualified deferred-compensation plans have clever names. One is the excess benefit or top-hat plan. This plan is used when the employer already has a qualified retirement plan and the limits on plan contributions and benefits are inadequate for the needs of highly compensated executives. An excess-benefit plan or top-hat plan provides additional tax-deferred retirement benefits for the executives. A supplemental employee retirement plan (SERP) is pretty much the same thing, except it might or might not be used in tandem with a qualified retirement plan.

Funding for these plans varies. Funds might be put in a separate account or trust owned by the employer, and the employer might purchase tax-exempt bonds, government securities, or other investments that it feels confident will help fund the promise to pay. Some employers buy insurance policies or endowment contracts to fund the promise. But there might not be any funding at all. The employer might merely promise to pay the compensation out of available cash flow when the payments are due.

The most common way of setting up a nonqualified deferred-compensation plan probably is the rabbi trust, so named because the first IRS ruling sanctioning this arrangement involved a synagogue that wanted to set up a nonqualified deferred-compensation plan for its rabbi. Under these plans the employer sets up a trust and makes contributions into it each year. The employer usually is the trustee and beneficiary and determines how the trust is invested. The trust keeps the assets safe from many of the employer's creditors, except in the case of the employer's bankruptcy and liquidation.

An additional advantage of many nonqualified deferred-compensation plans is that they typically pay a higher rate of return on your account than you could earn through traditional investments. This is possible because the corporation can invest for the long term and take advantage of some corporate investment tax shelters to boost the rate of return. The higher yield combined with the tax deferral is a strong incentive for an executive to receive some income through a nonqualified deferred compensation plan.

As with the nonqualified 401(k), the employer does not get a deduction until the employee recognizes income, and the employer is taxed on any income earned by the trust or account that funds the agreement.

Max decides to discuss having his bonuses and future salary increases structured as nonqualified deferred-compensation plans.

Split-Dollar Insurance

Another strategy Max's employer can help with is called split-dollar life insurance. It has been around for years, but it became more valuable because of the higher tax rates and additional pension restrictions of the Clinton tax code.

The strategy is that Max buys a cash value life insurance policy, but the employer pays the premiums. The only cost to Max is that he has to include in gross income the value of the term insurance portion of the premiums.

Max can use either of two methods to determine the cost of the term insurance. One method uses the rates for a standard term insurance policy available through the insurer. The other method uses tables issued by the IRS. The IRS tables usually but not always result in the lower cost. Or Max can avoid this tax by paying the portion of the premiums that are equal to the value of the term coverage.

After about ten years, the policy might be fully paid up and the employer could stop paying premiums. Income from the cash value would be sufficient to pay future premiums and still allow growth in the cash value and the insurance benefit over time.

Then Max has several options. He can simply let the policy continue as a benefit for his heirs. He can cash in the policy and add the after-tax cash value to his retirement fund. Or he can borrow against the cash value, usually up to 90 percent. Any loans do not have to be repaid and are nontaxable. But outstanding loans will reduce the death benefit available to Max's heirs. If Max borrows too much of the cash value, the policy might lapse. To avoid a lapse, Max would have to pay additional premiums or repay some of the loans. If the policy lapses, then Max must treat the outstanding loans as income in the year of the lapse.

There are several ways by which Max's employer eventually is repaid for the premiums. The employer could get a portion of the death benefit when Max dies, or the employer could borrow enough of the cash value after ten years or so to recoup the premiums. The employer also could cause the policy to be cashed in and could take its money from the proceeds. In the end, the employer essentially has made an interest-free loan to Max of the insurance premiums, so the only cost to the employer is the income it could have earned on the money.

The exact method of repayment is determined by Max and the employer at the outset and is included in the agreement.

Some split-dollar plans have a variation known as the rollout. After the policy has enough cash value to pay future premiums, the employer relinquishes its right to be repaid the premiums, and Max includes that amount in gross income. Max then owns a fully paid insurance policy with a substantial cash value and death benefit. And his cost is his tax rate times the premiums paid by the employer.

Note. Death benefits from a life insurance policy can avoid estate taxes if the policy is owned by an irrevocable life insurance trust. But if the policy is owned by a trust, you are not able to borrow against the cash value. So you need to decide at the outset whether you want to be able to take loans from the cash value.

Tax-Advantaged Investing

Max has tapped all the tax wise options his employer can offer to boost his retirement fund. Max and Rosie also have some investment funds. This portfolio will grow fatter and increase their after-tax wealth if Max and Rosie use investment strategies discussed elsewhere in this book, such as:

Tax-exempt investing. To provide some balance and diversity to their portfolio, Max and Rosie plan to invest in some fixed-income vehicles such as bonds. They plan to invest some of this in tax-exempt bonds.

Annuities. Variable and fixed-rate annuities are available to help the Profits build a retirement fund. There are no deductions for investments, but the income compounds tax-deferred.

Individual retirement accounts. Max can contribute up to $2,000 to an IRA each year. He will not be able to deduct the contributions because he is covered by a retirement plan at work. But after examining the power of tax-deferred compounding, Max now understands that $2,000 put into a nondeductible IRA each year can grow to a worthwhile number by the time he is ready to take the money out. Since Max plans to let the earnings compound for at least ten years, he is confident that the nondeductible IRA contributions will be big winners.

Capital gains investing. Max and Rosie will look for opportunities to earn long-term capital gains that will compound tax-deferred each year and eventually be taxed at a maximum rate of 28 percent. They also will take advantage of strategies that can reduce or eliminate taxes on capital gains.

Tax wise investing. In their taxable accounts, Max and Rosie plan to seek out tax wise mutual funds and any tax shelters that are appropriate for them.

Maximizing home equity. Home equity is the first or second most valuable asset available to most Americans. There are several ways in which the Profits can take advantage of their home equity.

Chapter 11

Taking Money from Retirement Plans

Employer pension plans and individual retirement accounts are among the most valuable assets most people own. Many of these plans have a wide range of bewildering options for withdrawing your money. There are few things more important to your retirement than understanding and carefully evaluating these options, because the difference could easily amount to tens of thousands of dollars or more over your retirement years.

In this chapter you will get an overview of the options available and the nontax factors to consider. You'll also learn how to avoid tax penalties on retirement plan distributions. In the next chapter you will learn how to maximize the after-tax cash you get from annuity and lump-sum distributions.

Tax wise money strategy. Begin planning your distributions well before you have to decide. First, get a list of the options available. Second, review the nontax factors, and use them to narrow down your choices. Third, compare the amount of money you would receive during your life expectancy from each of the remaining options.

Basic Distribution Options

The two basic retirement distribution options are an annuity or a lump-sum distribution. An annuity is a fixed periodic payment (usually made monthly). A lump sum is a payment of your entire retirement account balance.

Once you get beyond the basic options, each has variations and tax reporting options.

Annuity Options

With an annuity, you can select the period over which the annuity will be paid. The most common options are:

- a period certain (usually ten, fifteen, or twenty years);
- your life (single life annuity);
- the joint lives of you and a survivor, such as your spouse (joint life or joint and survivor annuity);
- life or joint life with a period certain.

Under the period certain, or life or joint life with period certain options, if you die before the period certain, your beneficiary receives the rest of the guaranteed payments.

The joint life or joint and survivor annuity has more options. You can choose to have same amount paid to your survivor as when you are alive (a joint and 100 percent survivor annuity). Or you can have the payout reduced after your death. The most common reduced payout options are 50 percent of the initial annuity (joint and 50 percent survivor) and 75 percent of the initial annuity (joint and 75 percent survivor).

The shorter the expected payout period, the larger each payment will be. Also, the amount of the annuity you leave for your surviving beneficiary will reduce the amount received during your lifetime. For example, here are the monthly payout options recently available to a married couple, each age sixty, with a $100,000 account value:

Single life	$ 789
Single life with 10 years certain	737
Joint life and 50% survivor	708
Joint life and 100% survivor	664
10 years certain	$1,077

There also are two ways of reporting an annuity on your tax return if you made after-tax contributions to the annuity. These options are explained in the next chapter.

Lump-sum options.

Once you decide to take a lump sum, the options are tax-reporting options. The main choices for reporting your lump sum on the tax return are:

- five-year averaging method;
- ten-year averaging method;

- capital gains treatment;
- IRA rollover;
- include in income with no special treatment.

The details of each of these options are in the next chapter.

Partial Lump Sum
Some retirement plans allow you to take part of the account balance in a lump sum and part as an annuity, known as a partial lump sum.

Note About IRAs
The lump sum distribution options apply only to qualified employer retirement plans. You can take an IRA or insurance annuity in a lump-sum distribution, but the special tax treatment will not be allowed. All IRA and annuity distributions, except those made with after-tax money, are taxed as ordinary income.

Nontax Factors to Consider

Maximizing after-tax cash is a goal. But there are other important factors to consider that might have nothing to do with taxes or directly affect the amount of cash you get. You need to consider these nontax issues as well as the tax issues.

Cash Needs
If you anticipate using the retirement account to meet a large cash need either at retirement or a few years later, then you should eliminate the annuity options. Possible large spending needs include medical expenses, a nursing home, major repairs to your home, or help for your children.

Purchasing Power
With few exceptions, pension plan and insurance annuities are not indexed for inflation. You get paid the same amount each period; meanwhile, your costs increase with inflation. At 4 percent inflation, the purchasing power of the payout is reduced by 25 percent after only eight years.

By taking a lump sum you have the opportunity to invest it to preserve your purchasing power. But if you do not have enough confidence in your investment ability to maintain purchasing power, you might opt for the certainty of the annuity.

Tax wise money strategy. A good approach for most people is to have a portion of their retirement income guaranteed as an annuity and the remainder in investment assets. For example, you can take a portion of the account as an annuity and the remainder as a lump sum. The annuity gives you the guaranteed floor, and the lump sum gives you an investment portfolio with which you can try to achieve a return that will beat inflation and taxes.

Simplifying Retirement

A lump-sum distribution can complicate your life because you take on the burden of investing the money. But an annuity puts this burden on an insurance company or the pension fund.

Also consider your spouse or other survivor. If you take a lump sum, what will happen to that investment fund if you die first? You could have the money paid to a trust or turned over to an investment manager after your death. You could direct your executor or surviving spouse to buy an annuity. Or you could take the annuity today.

Estate Planning

Your first concern is, of course, to provide for the needs of you and your spouse. But when your comfort seems secure, consider the effects your retirement account option has on your heirs.

When you choose a life annuity, there will be nothing left for your spouse or heirs. Your spouse will benefit if you choose a joint and survivor annuity, but your children or other heirs will not.

Also bear in mind that the value of pensions and IRAs is included in your estate. The only way to get retirement accounts out of your estate is to take distributions, pay the income taxes, then spend the money or give it to your heirs. In addition, when your heirs inherit a retirement account, they pay income taxes on the money as it is distributed from the account. So the money could be taxed twice: an estate tax at your death, and an income tax as your heirs receive the account balances. If you have a large retirement account, there also is a 15 percent excise tax imposed on "excess retirement accumulations" of $750,000 or more. That makes a potential third tax on your retirement assets after your death.

Longevity and Health

Healthy people from long-lived families tend to be fearful of outliving their assets. This situation makes a life or joint life annuity more attractive because you can't outlive it.

But if you have reason to believe that you might not live to your life expectancy, then consider a lump-sum distribution or an annuity for a fixed period.

An Option to Avoid

A strategy that can be packaged to look attractive but rarely is a good idea is pension maximization, or pension max.

Under pension max, instead of selecting a joint and survivor annuity, the retiree selects a single-life annuity. This gives the couple a higher income than under a joint and survivor annuity. But they do not use all the extra income for living expenses. Instead, they use at least part of the increased income to buy life insurance on the retiree's life for the spouse's benefit.

After the retiree dies, the annuity payments stop. But the life insurance proceeds are paid to the surviving spouse and can be used to buy another single-life annuity, presumably one that pays at least what the surviving spouse would have received under the joint and survivor annuity option.

When presented like this, the proposal sounds good. But there are several problems.

Example. A couple could take a single-life pension of $2,957 a month or a joint and 100% survivor monthly pension of $2,306. That's a $651 difference. The pension max recommendation was to take the single-life annuity and buy life insurance for a $585 monthly premium. This left the couple with an extra $66 per month while they were both alive. The insurance proceeds after the death of the retiree would be enough to buy an annuity paying the spouse $1,679 monthly. That is significantly less than under the joint and 100 percent survivor annuity. Therefore, to make these numbers look attractive, the presentation pointed out that the joint life annuity would be taxed and would pay only $1,660 to the surviving spouse after taxes.

Problems with pension max. Unfortunately, the presentation overlooked a few facts. First, the proposal failed to point out that the annuity purchased by the surviving spouse with the life insurance proceeds also would be taxed, leaving less spending money than under the projections. In addition, the single-life annuity taken by the retiree also would be taxed. That means there really would not be enough money after taxes to buy the life insurance policy. In short, when income taxes are taken completely into account, the numbers do not add up.

An additional problem is that pension max proposals usually recommend universal life insurance, because universal life starts with lower premiums than traditional whole-life policies. But the death benefit and premiums are not fixed. If interest rates fall after the purchase, as they did from 1982 through 1993, the policyholder has to find additional cash to put into the insurance policy, let it lapse, or let the death benefit be reduced.

This is quite a gamble to take with your retirement income, and your surviving spouse's.

Falling interest rates also can cut the surviving spouse's income under pension max. The pension max presentation assumes that the life insurance benefits will purchase an annuity paying a certain amount. But the payout of an annuity depends on the interest rates that prevail when the annuity is purchased. If you make your assumptions when interest rates are high but your spouse has to buy an annuity when interest rates are low, the payout from the annuity will be much lower than projected.

Pension max can work effectively if you start paying for the life insurance about fifteen years before retirement. Then you can buy a more substantial insurance policy so that the surviving spouse comes out clearly ahead. But if you wait until retirement, it is difficult to make pension max work.

Boost Annuity Income 20 Percent

When you decide to annuitize either your pension account or an insurance annuity, do not settle for the annuity offered by your employer or insurer. Payouts for the same individual differ greatly among insurance companies. Get quotes for immediate annuities from several insurance companies. You might increase retirement income by 20 percent or more by using the account to purchase an immediate annuity instead of taking the annuity your current account offers. For details, see the chapter on tax-deferred investing through insurance.

Avoiding Penalties on Retirement Distributions

Penalties are imposed for taking distributions too early or too late in life, or for distributions that are too small or too large. The penalties are in addition to any regular income tax. The penalties for early distributions also are imposed on insurance annuities.

But the penalties can be avoided. You should be able to plan and manage your distributions in many cases to avoid the penalties.

As far as the tax code is concerned, there are three time periods in which retirement distributions might be taken:

- before age 59½;
- between ages 59½ and 70½;
- after age 70½.

Withdrawals Before Age 59½

Retirement plan distributions before age 59½ are "early distributions" and are subject to a 10 percent penalty unless you qualify for one of several exceptions.

The penalty on early withdrawals applies to distributions from IRAs; qualified retirement plans, including 401(k)s; and insurance annuities. When your account is used as collateral or security for a loan, that is treated as a withdrawal.

The early withdrawal penalty is not always onerous enough to discourage early withdrawals or even to discourage the use of IRAs or qualified plans when you know the money will be needed before age 59½. If you let the income and gains compound long enough, a retirement account or IRA is better than a taxable account even if you withdraw the money before age 59½ and pay the 10 percent penalty.

Example. You earn 8 percent on your money before taxes and have $2,000 that could be put in either a taxable account or in an IRA. If you can deduct the IRA contribution and are able to leave the money in the IRA for eight years before withdrawing it, you will have roughly the same after-tax cash as you would have accumulated in a taxable account—even after paying the 10 percent penalty. This assumes that you save and invest the tax savings you get from deducting the IRA contribution. If you can let the money accumulate in the IRA longer, you come out ahead of the taxable account even after the 10 percent penalty. When after-tax (nondeductible) contributions are put in an IRA (or you do not save and invest the tax savings from a deductible contribution), you need to let the income compound for at least thirteen years to have the same after-tax cash as with a taxable account.

Early Distributions Penalty-Free

There are several exceptions to the 10 percent early withdrawal penalty, but only one of these provides tax planning opportunities.

Substantially Equal Payments

The early distribution penalty is avoided if the money is withdrawn in "substantially equal annual installments." This basically requires you to begin taking an annuity from your IRA, insurance annuity, or other retirement account. Look at how this exception works, as described in one IRS ruling.

Checklist for Avoiding Early Distribution Penalty

A distribution from a qualified retirement plan, IRA, or insurance annuity generally is subject to a 10 percent early distribution penalty if you received it before age 59½. But if you can answer "yes" to any of the following questions, you do not owe the penalty.

Yes   No

_____ _____ Were you age 59½ or older at the time of the distribution?

_____ _____ Was the distribution from a qualified employer retirement plan, and were you disabled at the time of the distribution?

_____ _____ Was the distribution from a qualified employer retirement plan, and did you receive the distribution as the beneficiary of a deceased employee?

_____ _____ Was the distribution one of a series of substantially equal payments to be made over a period of at least your life expectancy or the joint life expectancy of you and a beneficiary?

_____ _____ Was the distribution from an employee stock ownership plan that met the five-year investment requirement?

_____ _____ Was the distribution made under a qualified domestic relations order?

_____ _____ Was the distribution rolled over into an IRA or another qualified retirement plan within sixty days of your receiving it?

_____ _____ Were you over age fifty-four, and did you receive the distribution as part of a qualified early retirement payment?

_____ _____ Was the distribution made from a qualified employer retirement plan and used to pay medical expenses that exceed 7.5 percent of adjusted gross income?

Example. Max Profits left his employer at age forty-five, taking a lump sum of $1.2 million in retirement benefits, which he rolled over to an IRA. After five years Max decides to make $250,000 of improvements to his home when his IRA is a little over $1.8 million. If he withdrew a lump sum to pay for the improvements, he would have to withdraw more than $400,000 to have $250,000 left after paying both income taxes and the 10 percent penalty.

As an alternative, Max took out a fifteen-year second mortgage on the home. The monthly mortgage payments at the time were $3,000.42, for a yearly total of $36,005 in principal and interest. To make the mortgage payments, Max takes substantially equal periodic withdrawals of $55,781 from the IRA and uses the after-tax proceeds to make the mortgage payments. Max also deducts interest paid on the mortgage.

So Max pays for the improvements over time, uses the IRA distributions to make the mortgage payments, avoids the 10 percent penalty, and deducts interest on the mortgage payments. In addition, if Max's IRA is able to earn investment returns that are greater than the rate at which he is taking withdrawals, the IRA balance will grow during the fifteen years.

Important caveat. Max did not pledge the IRA as collateral for the mortgage or take any other step that could be construed as using the IRA as security for the mortgage. If he had, the entire $250,000 would be treated as a distribution to Max in the year the mortgage was signed.

To qualify for this exception, distributions must be taken at least annually. The payments must be scheduled to last for your life expectancy or the joint life expectancy of you and a beneficiary. And the distributions must continue until the later of either five years or when you reach age 59½. That means that if you begin periodic payments at age 57, they must last at least 5 years. If you begin the payments at age 50, they must continue until age 59½. After you have continued the payments for the required minimum period, you can stop receiving payments under the schedule.

The IRS has approved three ways for computing the substantially equal periodic payments.

Straight life expectancy. In life expectancy tables issued by the IRS, you locate the appropriate life expectancy for you (or you and your beneficiary) and divide that number into the IRA account balance. The result is the distribution for the year.

Example. Under Table V, a 50-year-old has a life expectancy of 33.1 years. If the account has a balance of $100,000, the annual payout is $3,021.15.

You can recalculate the life expectancy each year if you want, and that will change the amount distributed.

Amortization method. You assume a reasonable rate of interest and a period of years equal to your life expectancy. Then you use a financial calculator or amortization tables to compute the distributions.

Example. If you have a $100,000 IRA, assume an 8 percent interest rate, and a 33.1-year life expectancy, the distribution is $8,679 annually.

Some advisers believe that you should be able to adjust the interest rate annually, as with an adjustable-rate mortgage, and recompute the life expectancy annually, as with the required minimum payment, but the IRS has not taken a clear position on these issues.

Annuity method. Look up your life expectancy in any reasonable mortality tables; determine a reasonable interest rate; and, using these figures, go to a standard annuity table and determine the payment factor. The payment factor is divided into the IRA account balance to determine your annual distributions.

Example. If you have a $100,000 account balance, are 50 years old, use the UP-1984 mortality tables, and use an 8 percent interest rate, the annuity factor is 11.109. This gives you an annual distribution of $9,002.

You can see that the three methods can give very different results:

Straight-line	$3,021.15
Amortization	$8,679.00
Annuitization	$9,002.00

You can choose the method that best meets your needs.

The Middle Years and "Dribble Out" Distributions

When you are between ages 59½ and 70½, you have total discretion over how much money to take and when to take it. Or you can decide not to withdraw any money during this period. (But an employer plan or IRA might impose its own restrictions.)

Distributions during this period sometimes are known as "dribble out" distributions. The only tax effect is that distributions are included in your gross income. If you have an employer pension plan, double-check to be sure that any "dribble out" distributions you take do not make you ineligible for favored lump-sum treatment down the road.

Tax wise money strategy. When you do not need the money, in most cases the best move is to let the income and gains compound tax-deferred.

Avoiding the Success Tax

A 15 percent excise tax is imposed on "excess retirement distributions or accumulations.'' If you take annual distributions that exceed approximately $150,000, the excess amount is hit with a 15 percent excise tax in addition to the regular income tax. Or if you take a lump distribution that exceeds approximately $750,000, that excess is hit with the excise tax. If you leave the money in your retirement plans for your heirs, your estate will be hit with the 15 percent tax for excess pension accumulations, in addition to the regular estate tax, for accumulations exceeding about $750,000. (These amounts are indexed for inflation.)

Tax wise money strategy. One way to avoid this tax is to take distributions that exceed your cash needs and are less than $150,000 annually. You might be better off taking the money now and paying the regular income tax instead of letting the retirement fund grow so it is hit with the 15 percent penalty tax. Another option is to provide for the 15 percent tax on your estate by purchasing life insurance. You can defer the problem by naming your spouse as beneficiary of the retirement account and instructing him or her to avoid the 15 percent tax on your estate by electing to have the retirement account subject to the tax as part of his or her estate. Then your spouse can spend down the account or buy insurance to take care of the penalty tax.

Required Retirement Distributions

After you reach age 70½, you must begin minimum annual distributions from your retirement plans or pay a substantial penalty. (Required minimum distributions do not apply to insurance annuities.) The penalty is an excise tax of 50 percent of the amount that was supposed to be distributed.

Financial institutions and retirement plan sponsors are not required to make the distributions automatically. Many of them will contact you when you turn age 70, remind you of the rules, and give you a form to get the payments started. But it is up to you to see that the distributions are made for at least the required minimum amount.

Tax wise money strategy. The first required payment must be made no later than April 1 of the year following the year in which you turn age 70½. After the first required payment, minimum distributions must be made by December 31 of each year. So if you wait to take the first distribution until April 1 of the year following the year you turn age 70½, you will have two required distributions that year: the initial required distribution, taken on April 1; and the second year's required distribution, which must be taken by December 31. A better strategy is to take the first required distribution by December 31 of the year that you turn age 70½.

You can take the required distributions in any pattern during the year as long as the total distributions by the end of the year at least equal the required minimum amount. You also can take more than the required minimum in a year.

Example. Max Profits' birthday was June 30, 1923. That means he turned 70 on June 30, 1993, and 70½ on December 30, 1993. His distributions must begin by April 1, 1994. But if Max's birthday were July 1, 1923, he would turn 70 on July 1, 1993, and 70½ on January 1, 1994. His required distributions would not have to begin until April 1, 1995.

Calculating Minimum Distributions

The minimum distributions may be calculated over any one of the following periods:

- Your life expectancy;
- the joint life expectancy of you and a designated beneficiary;
- a fixed period that does not extend beyond your life expectancy;
- a fixed period that does not extend beyond the joint life expectancy of you and a designated beneficiary.

Therefore, one way to stretch out the payments is to use the joint life expectancy of you and a beneficiary who is younger than you are. But there are limits to make sure your choice of beneficiary does not stretch out the payments too far.

To determine the required distribution for a year, start with the value of your account as of the close of business on December 31 of the preceding year. The year-end value is divided by your applicable life expectancy from the IRS's life expectancy tables, which are contained in IRS Publications 575 and 590 and in regulations Section 1.72-9.

Annual recalculation. After the first year, you can choose from either of two methods for calculating the rest of the required minimum distributions. Under one method you simply subtract "1" from the previous year's life expectancy and divide that remainder into the account balance at the end of the previous year. Under the other method you return to the life expectancy tables and find your new life expectancy. This is known as recalculating life expectancy.

Tax wise money strategy. Recalculating the life expectancy each year generally reduces the minimum distributions, makes the retirement account last longer, and maximizes the use of tax-deferred compounding. That is because each year you live increases your life expectancy.

Beneficiaries and Required Distributions

When you designate a beneficiary other than your spouse, a special rule comes into play to make sure you do not reduce your required minimum distributions too much. When the beneficiary is much younger than you, the required distributions are computed using the joint life expectancy of you and a hypothetical individual who is no more than ten years younger than you. If the beneficiary is less than ten years younger than you, the actual joint life expectancy of the two of you is used.

Tax wise money strategy. If your spouse already is provided for, consider designating someone other than your spouse and who is younger than you as the beneficiary of your IRA or retirement plan. This designation allows you to reduce the required minimum distributions. Appropriate beneficiaries are children and grandchildren.

Tax wise money strategy. Do not designate a revocable or living trust as the beneficiary of your IRA. When a revocable trust is the beneficiary of your IRA, after you die, the entire account balance must be paid out the following year. That means that all the income is taxable to the beneficiary in one year; the benefits of tax deferral are lost.

Chapter 12

Tax Options for Annuities and Lump Sums

After examining the basic differences between annuities and lump sums, it is time to look at the tax-reporting options. Annuities can be reported in two ways on your tax return, and lump sums have even more options. Here's how to make your choice.

Tax Options for Annuities

From a tax standpoint there are two types of annuities: those to which you made after-tax contributions, and those to which you did not. An after-tax contribution is one made from money on which income taxes already have been paid.

No after-tax contributions. When you did not make any after-tax contributions to the annuity account, the tax treatment is very simple: You include the entire amount of each annuity payment in your gross income. That is because you were not previously taxed on any of the money in the account.

After-tax contributions. You are not taxed when after-tax contributions are returned to you. Part of each annuity payment will be considered a tax-free return of your after-tax contributions, and part will be a taxable receipt of earnings, employer contributions, and your pretax contributions.

The IRS gives you two options for computing the tax-free portion: the exclusion method and the safe-harbor method. They are described in Publication 575. The exclusion method not only is more complicated (you have to look up your life expectancy in IRS tables and make several calculations), but it also results in a higher tax for most people.

Tax wise money strategy. Many people can save tax dollars (not to mention time and tax preparation fees) each year by using the safe-harbor method instead of the exclusion method. For the best results, compute your tax both ways the first year you receive an annuity, then use the most favorable method every year after that.

Maximizing Lump-Sum Distributions

If you choose a lump-sum distribution from your retirement plan, you can choose to report it on your tax return under one of the following methods:

- five-year averaging;
- ten-year averaging;
- capital gains treatment;
- IRA rollover;
- ordinary income.

But not everyone can use each of these options.

Use the next few sections of this chapter to determine which lump-sum methods are available to you. Then use the remainder of the chapter to maximize the after-tax wealth you will get from the lump sum.

What Is a Lump Sum?

To be considered a lump-sum distribution under the tax law, and to be eligible for an averaging method or capital gains treatment, a pension plan distribution must meet these requirements:

1. The payment must be from a qualified pension, profit-sharing, or stock bonus plan.

2. The lump sum must be all of the money to which you are entitled under the plan. When you are a participant under more than one plan with different employers, this rule generally applies separately to each plan. Different types of plans with the same employer—such as pension and 401(k) plans—also are treated as separate plans under this rule.

3. All the money from the plan must be received by you within one of your taxable years, which usually is a calendar year. There can be more than one payment. **Note:** The year you retire does not have to be the year the lump sum is received.

4. You must meet at least one of the following conditions at the time of the distribution:
- You are at least age 59½ (unless you were at least age fifty by January 1, 1986).
- You are separated from the service of the employer.
- You are a self-employed individual or an owner-employee who is disabled.

5. You were a participant in the retirement plan for at least five years before the distribution.

IRA rollover safe harbor. If you do not meet all the above requirements, you are not eligible to use an averaging method or to elect capital gains treatment on your lump-sum payment. But you can roll over the distribution to an individual retirement account within sixty days of receiving the distribution. But to avoid the 20 percent withholding tax described in the previous chapter, an IRA rollover should be done by having the trustee of your pension plan transfer the lump sum directly to the IRA trustee.

Separation from service. Separation from service generally means you retired, resigned, or were discharged. The IRS often says that a taxpayer is not "separated from the service of an employer" and is not eligible for lump-sum distribution treatment when he or she has a consulting agreement or some kind of part-time role with the former employer. The IRS is successful with this argument when the consulting work is substantial, the retiree has an ownership interest in the employer, or the retiree does not have other clients.

Tax wise money strategy. If you want to get lump-sum treatment on your distribution while having a consulting arrangement with the employer, be sure to limit the scope of the consulting. At a minimum, you should not have an assigned office or desk at the employer's office, the time commitment should be relatively small, and you should try to develop consulting work elsewhere.

The Averaging Methods

The five-year and ten-year lump-sum averaging methods sometimes are known as forward averaging because their intent is more or less to impose the same tax you would pay if you received the money in equal installments over five or ten years. Each averaging method has different qualifications for using it.

Checklist for Special Averaging for Lump Sums

This checklist will help you determine if you are eligible to use either five-year or ten-year special averaging on your retirement plan distribution. To use an averaging method you must answer "yes" to each of the following questions.

Yes	No	
_____	_____	Was the distribution from a qualified pension, profit-sharing, or stock bonus plan? This does not include a distribution from an IRA, tax-sheltered annuity under Section 403(b), or a Section 457 plan.
_____	_____	Did you receive the entire balance of your account within one taxable year?
_____	_____	Were you a participant in the qualified plan for at least five years?
_____	_____	Can you answer "yes" to at least one of the following? Was the distribution made because you separated from the service of your employer? Were you at least age 59½ at the time of the distribution? Did you become disabled before the distribution, and were you either self-employed or an owner-employee? Did you receive the distribution as the beneficiary of an employee who died?
_____	_____	If you used averaging previously, was the averaging used before 1987, were you under age 59½ at that time, and were you at least age fifty by January 1, 1986? To use ten-year averaging you also must be able to answer "yes" to the following question:
_____	_____	Were you at least age fifty by January 1, 1986?

Five-Year Averaging

If you were born before January 1, 1936, you can use five-year averaging at any point in your life. Taxpayers born after that date can use five-year averaging only if the lump sum is received after age 59½, unless the lump sum was received because of death or disability.

Five-year averaging generally is a once-in-a-lifetime election. Someone who elected ten-year averaging on a lump sum received before 1987 and who was under age 59½ at the time can make another averaging election in the future. But for other taxpayers, five-year averaging can be used only once in their lifetimes.

Ten-Year Averaging

Ten-year averaging is available only to taxpayers who were born before January 1, 1936, and under the same once-a-lifetime limit as five-year averaging. That means that if you used averaging on a pre-1987 lump sum and were under age 59½ at the time, you can use averaging one more time. Otherwise you can use ten-year averaging only once.

Computing and Reporting Averaging

Computing the tax under averaging is fairly simple. Form 4972 is used to compute and report lump-sum averaging in the year of the distribution. The form has a series of questions you must answer to ensure that the distribution qualifies as a lump sum and that you are eligible for averaging.

Ten-Year Formula

To compute the tax under ten-year averaging, subtract from the lump sum any after-tax contributions you made. Also subtract any amount for which you plan to take the capital gains option (described later in this chapter). You also can subtract a "minimum distribution allowance" if your lump sum is less than $70,000. The allowance is $10,000, but it is reduced by 20 percent of the amount by which the distribution exceeds $20,000.

Take 10 percent of the remaining amount of the lump sum and compute the tax for a single taxpayer with no dependents under the 1986 tax tables. Use the single-taxpayer tables regardless of your actual filing status. In the past, before consulting the tax table you first had to add the 1986 zero bracket amount (similar to the standard deduction of today) for a single taxpayer, of $2,480. But in the instructions for Form 4972 the IRS issued new 1986 tax tables incorporating the zero bracket amount. So don't subtract the zero bracket amount unless you use the original 1986 tax tables.

After determining the tax for a single taxpayer in 1986, multiply by 10; that is your tax for the lump sum under ten-year averaging.

Example. You receive a lump sum distribution of $150,000 in 1994. No capital gains tax treatment is elected for any portion, the lump sum is not eligible for the minimum distribution allowance, and there are no after-tax employee contributions in the lump sum. You calculate that 10 percent of the lump sum is $15,000. In the 1986 tax tables, the tax for a single taxpayer with no dependents is $2,457. Multiply this tax by 10 and get $24,570 as the tax on your lump sum under ten-year averaging.

Five-Year Formula

Five-year averaging uses the same basic steps as ten-year averaging, except you take 20 percent of your lump sum after subtractions instead

Table 1
Lump-Sum Averaging Methods: Comparison of Tax Burdens

	50,000	100,000	150,000	200,000	300,000	400,000	500,000	600,000	700,000
Lump-sum amount	50,000	100,000	150,000	200,000	300,000	400,000	500,000	600,000	700,000
Minimum distribution allowance	4,000								
Amount to be taxed	46,000	100,000	150,000	200,000	300,000	400,000	500,000	600,000	700,000

Ten-Year Averaging: 1986 Rates

10% of amount to be taxed plus $2,480	7,080	12,480	17,480	22,480	32,480	42,480	52,480	62,480	72,480
Tax @ 1986 single rates	587	1,437	2,536	3,691	6,631	10,258	14,368	18,737	23,537
Tax × 10 = total tax	5,870	14,370	25,360	36,910	66,310	102,580	143,680	187,370	235,370
Tax rate on total distribution	12%	14%	17%	18%	22%	26%	29%	31%	34%

Five-Year Averaging: 1994 Rates

20% of amount to be taxed	9,200	20,000	30,000	40,000	60,000	80,000	100,000	120,000	140,000
Tax @ 1994 single rates	1,380	3,000	5,443	8,243	13,990	20,190	26,390	32,840	40,040
1994 tax × 5 = total tax	6,900	15,000	27,213	41,213	69,948	100,948	131,948	164,198	200,198
Tax rate on total distribution	14%	15%	18%	21%	23%	25%	26%	27%	29%

of 10 percent, and capital gains treatment is not allowed for any portion of the lump sum. Also, you use the current-year tax tables for a single taxpayer with no dependents. After determining the tax on 20 percent of the lump sum, multiply by 5 to get the tax on your lump sum.

Example. You receive a $150,000 lump sum in 1994. You take 20 percent of this and get $30,000. Under the 1994 tax tables, the tax for a single taxpayer with no dependents is $5,422.50. Multiply by 5; the tax on your lump sum using five-year averaging is $27,212.50.

Tax wise money strategy. Ten-year averaging always uses the 1986 tax tables, while five-year averaging always uses the current-year tax tables. That means that for five-year averaging the tables are inflation-indexed, and the tax on the same lump sum using five-year averaging is going to be lower in one year than it would have been the previous year. For example, the tax on the $150,000 lump sum in 1993 would have been $27,635. You would have saved $422.50 by delaying the lump sum from 1993 to 1994. If you have decided to use five-year averaging and are thinking of taking the lump sum late in the year, why not wait until the following January when the tax tables are indexed and save a few dollars?

Capital Gains Treatment

The capital gains option generally was abolished in the Tax Reform Act of 1986. A grandfather provision, however, allows benefits earned before 1974 to be taxed at a 20 percent rate to taxpayers who were born before January 1, 1936 and who use ten-year averaging to report the rest of the distribution. The computation of pre-1974 benefits is generous. You assume benefits were earned evenly over your years of service. So if half of your years of service with a firm were before 1974, you can apply capital gains treatment to half of your lump-sum distribution.

IRA Rollover

The requirements for an IRA rollover are that the distribution must be from a qualified retirement plan, and the rollover must be completed within sixty days of your receiving the distribution. Any after-tax employee contributions in a distribution must be deducted before a rollover is made. There are no age restrictions, minimum service requirements, or even a requirement that you be separated from the service of the employer. An IRA rollover can be done if less than your entire retirement account balance is distributed.

There are two ways to do an IRA rollover. One way is for you to receive a check from the retirement plan and deposit an amount equal to the distribution in an IRA or other employee plan within sixty days. If you miss the sixty-day deadline, the entire amount of the distribution is included in your gross income even if it is deposited in an IRA after the sixty-day deadline.

The other method is to have your retirement plan administrator transfer your account balance directly to an IRA designated by you; often this is called a trustee-to-trustee transfer. Because the pension fund must withhold 20 percent of your lump sum if the check is made out to you, the trustee-to-trustee transfer is by far the best way to execute an IRA rollover. Otherwise you have to come up with enough cash to equal the 20 percent withholding and deposit that in the IRA with the 80 percent of the lump sum that was not withhold.

Comparing Averaging Methods

There are two key differences between the averaging methods. The obvious difference is that one method assumes the income was spread over ten years, while the other assumes it was earned over five years.

The more important difference is that ten-year averaging uses the 1986 tax tables, while five-year averaging uses the current tax tables. The 1986 tables have fifteen tax brackets, with marginal tax rates ranging from 11 percent to 50 percent. After the 1993 tax hike, the current tables have five tax brackets, with marginal rates ranging from 15 percent to 39.6 percent.

Tax wise money strategy. The effect of the different tax tables is that for smaller lump sums, ten-year averaging results in a lower tax. But as the amount of the lump sum gets higher, five-year averaging imposes a lower tax. Smaller lump sums are favored by ten-year averaging because the 1986 tax tables start with a lower tax rate and take longer to get to the top rate. But larger lump sums are favored by the current tax tables because the current tax tables have a much lower top tax rate than the 1986 tables. The crossover point when five-year averaging is better than ten-year averaging currently is reached when a lump sum is between $300,000 and $400,000. The exact crossover point changes each year because the current tax tables are indexed for inflation. Table 1 in this chapter shows the taxes due in 1994 under both averaging methods for lump-sum distributions of different amounts.

IRA Pros and Cons

An IRA rollover has two powerful tools in its favor: The first is that there is no current tax on the distribution; the second is that the earnings of your IRA compound tax-deferred until withdrawn.

The disadvantages of an IRA rollover are that you only get to spend the IRA money by paying taxes on it, and IRA distributions are taxed as ordinary income. You cannot use an averaging method or capital gains treatment.

Bringing It All Together

So far you've learned the general advantages and disadvantages of each method. Which produces the most after-tax wealth in your case?

Many taxpayers and financial advisers rely on general rules when evaluating retirement distribution options. They assert, for example, that an IRA always is better because of the tax deferral or that averaging is better because IRA withdrawals are taxed as ordinary income.

Tax wise money strategy. Avoid the temptation to use general rules. You have only one retirement and unique circumstances. To maximize after-tax retirement wealth you (or your adviser) should make projections on a computer spreadsheet that fit your circumstances. This is relatively easy and inexpensive to do with today's technology. Or you can do the projections the old-fashioned way using a sheet of paper, a calculator, and a pencil.

Before doing a comparison, be sure all the facts are gathered. You need to know the amount of your lump sum, which annuity option you favor, and the annuity your pension plan would pay under that option. Ideally you also have shopped around among some insurance companies to get an idea of competitive payouts from immediate annuities.

Then you need to make some assumptions about your future: tax rates, the rate of return on your investments, the average rate of inflation during retirement, and the withdrawal or spending schedule you would use under the IRA rollover and averaging options. Your best move is to make three sets of projections using different assumptions: best case, worst case, and most likely case.

Remember that an IRA rollover is best if you take advantage of the power of tax-deferred compounding. So if you have other investments and sources of income, you can assume that a lump sum is rolled over into an IRA and allowed to compound for several years before any withdrawals are made.

The following analysis compares an annuity with the different lump-sum options. It also presents two different spending schedules. Under one schedule, spending from the lump sum begins immediately. Under the second schedule, spending from the lump-sum distribution does not begin for five years.

Example. Max Profits and his wife, Rosie, are both age sixty-five. Max is about to retire, and his employer said that he can take either a $350,000 lump sum or an annuity. Max and Rosie decide that if they take an annuity it will be a joint and 100 percent survivor annuity, which the employer says would be $32,000 annually. The Profits check with several insurance companies and decide that the employer is offering them the best deal.

The Profits estimate that they will be in a combined average federal and state bracket of 20 percent after retirement. This would give them $25,600 after taxes from the annuity. They also estimate that if they take a lump sum they can earn an average 9 percent pretax return, and believe that inflation will average about 4 percent during their retirement years. The portion of the lump sum eligible for capital gains treatment is $100,000.

Table 2 is a summary of the results the Profits would get from these assumptions. Under the lump-sum options, the annual spending increases with the rate of inflation to maintain their standard of living.

Analyzing the Results

The results for Max and Rosie show that under these assumptions the IRA rollover is better than the averaging options. In addition, the results for both the IRA rollover and the averaging options are improved when you let distributions compound for five years before beginning withdrawals.

A potential advantage of the annuity is that its return is fairly certain. The projections for the IRA rollover and the averaging method are based on the assumption that Max and Rosie can earn 9 percent before taxes on their investments. But it is not certain that the Profits will earn that 9 percent. That is why the Profits should see what the numbers look like under lower returns. If the results assuming a lower return are not clearly better than the annuity, or if the Profits are not confident of their ability to invest well, they might opt for the certainty of the annuity.

The big disadvantage of the annuity is that there is no way to preserve purchasing power. You take the risk that inflation might accelerate after you agree to the fixed income. Even if inflation remains at its current 3 percent to 4 percent rate, the Profits' standard of living will erode significantly after ten years.

What if tax rates rise? That would seem to take the advantage away from the IRA rollover, since it defers taxes, but the averaging method pays them up front. But an IRA rollover still can be the best choice despite higher future tax rates if the money is allowed to compound for at least five years before distributions begin.

The Partial-Lump-Sum Option

Suppose you want some but not all of your retirement income guaranteed. A solution is to use both an annuity and an IRA rollover. The tax law provides for this option by allowing partial-lump-sum distributions.

Table 2
Summary of Retirement Distribution Options

Name: Max Profits
Lump-Sum Amount: $350,000
Average Tax Rate: 20%
Inflation Rate: 4%

Option	Initial Tax	Net Sum Invested	Income at Age 65*	Income at Age 75*	Balance at Age 75	Age When Income Ends
Pension annuity (no COLA)	0	0	$32,000 $25,600	$21,275 $17,020	0	Death
10-year avg./imm. distr.	$70,770	$279,230	$32,000 $25,600	$32,000 $25,600	$112,670	78
5-year avg./imm. distr.	$60,106	$256,890	$32,000 $25,600	$32,000 $25,600	$95,677	77
IRA rollover/imm. distr.	0	$350,000	$32,000 $25,600	$32,000 $25,600	$260,821	82
IRA rollover/5-year delay	0	$350,000	0 0	$32,000 $25,600	$577,878	96
10-year avg./5-year delay	$70,770	$299,335	0 0	$32,000 $25,600	$365,898	87

*Pretax amount on first line and after-tax amount on second line, adjusted to 1994 purchasing power, assuming 4% annual inflation.

Chart 1
Rollover vs. 10-Year Averaging
Annual Distributions Delayed 5 Years

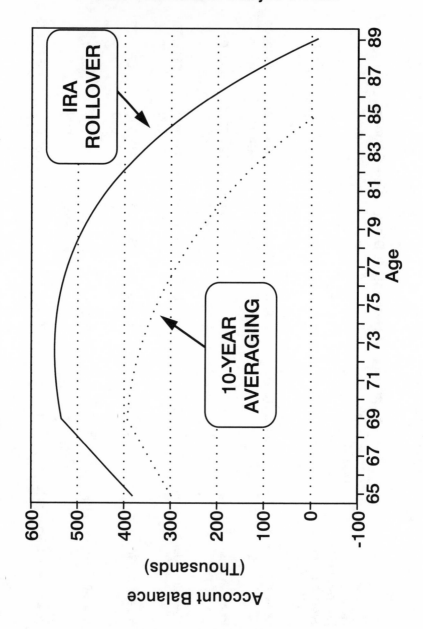

A partial lump sum is a distribution of any amount less than 100 percent of your retirement account. You can take a partial lump sum when you are over age 59½ or when the distribution occurs after your disability or death. When a distribution qualifies as a partial lump sum, you can roll over the lump-sum portion into an IRA just as you would a full lump sum, but you cannot use an averaging method.

Once you take a partial lump-sum distribution, the remaining amount in your retirement plan can be taken at any time as either an IRA rollover or as an annuity.

Another approach that yields similar results is to have your employer use part of your retirement account to purchase an annuity contract. Then have the entire account—both the annuity contract and the cash balance—distributed to you as a lump sum. In this case the averaging methods or an IRA rollover can be used with the cash. With the annuity, the payments are taxed to you as you receive them, just as other annuity payments are taxed.

Chapter 13

Taking Those Impossible Deductions: Miscellaneous Expenses

The grab bag of deductions for individual taxpayers is the category called "miscellaneous itemized expenses." This includes unreimbursed employment-related expenses, investment expenses, and tax-planning and preparation expenses.

To be deductible, investment expenses must be ordinary and necessary for at least one of the following:

- the production or collection of income;
- the management, conservation, or maintenance of property held for the production of income;
- the determination, collection, or refund of any tax. The main categories of expenses are investment, employment, and tax-related expenses.

Impossible Deductions?

Many people believe that it is impossible to take miscellaneous itemized expense deductions, because you can deduct only the expenses that exceed 2 percent of adjusted gross income.

Example. You have adjusted gross income of $50,000. You get no tax benefit from the first $1,000 of miscellaneous itemized expenses, and get a deduction only if your total miscellaneous expenses exceed $1,000.

Some miscellaneous expenses are deductible without regard to the 2 percent floor. These deductions include impairment-related work expenses of the handicapped; estate taxes related to income in respect of a decedent;

amortizable bond premiums; expenses of short sales in the nature of interest; and gambling losses to the extent of winnings.

But the checklist in this chapter shows you how many ordinary expenses qualify for this deduction. Most people do not take this deduction because they do not keep good records or do not realize how many expenses qualify for the deduction. In this chapter you'll also learn strategies for increasing the amount of your deduction.

AMT alert. Many itemized deductions are not allowed if you are subject to the alternative minimum tax. Do not maximize itemized deductions in a year when you might be subject to the AMT.

For Itemizers Only

You can deduct miscellaneous itemized expenses only if you itemize deductions on Schedule A. To do that, your total itemized expenses need exceed the standard deduction amount.

The standard deduction for the different filing statuses in 1994 was:

Married filing jointly	$6,350
Heads of households	5,600
Unmarried individuals	3,800
Married filing separately	3,175

Itemized-Deduction Reduction

As part of the 1993 tax law's assault on "the rich," itemized expense deductions are reduced for taxpayers whose adjusted gross incomes are "too high." Under the itemized-deduction reduction, your itemized deductions are reduced by 3 percent of the amount by which your adjusted gross income exceeds the threshold amount. For 1994 the threshold amounts were $111,800 for most taxpayers, and $55,900 for married taxpayers filing separately.

You cannot lose more than 80 percent of your itemized deductions under this provision. In addition, itemized deductions exempt from the reduction are medical expenses, investment interest, casualty losses, and wagering losses to the extent of wagering gains.

Impossible Expense Strategies

Before looking at specific deductions, let's look at two strategies for maximizing your deductions for these expenses.

Bunching Boosts Deductions

Bunching is paying as many deductible expenses in one year as possible, then paying as few as possible the following year. You estimate the expenses you are likely to incur over the next two years and plan to get as many as possible into one tax year. To bunch expenses, you have to schedule carefully when services are performed or goods are purchased and also control when payments are made. Here's an example of bunching expenses:

Example. Max Profits subscribes to a number of investment magazines and newsletters. Max subscribes for one year in January 1995 and pays for one-year renewals in December 1995. This puts two years of deductions in 1995. In 1996 Max will have no subscription expenses to deduct, and he will begin the cycle again in January 1997.

Caution. The IRS prohibits deductions for prepayment of goods and services that will be received substantially beyond the year of payment. So you should not pay for a two- or three-year subscription in 1995 and deduct the entire amount in 1995. You cannot deduct a payment for a service until the service has been provided or you are legally required to make the payment.

Can't Beat the Floor? Reclassify

Suppose you think it is unlikely that you will be able to deduct miscellaneous expenses because of the floor. Consider classifying the expenses in another deductible category.

For example, if you receive financial publications that could be attributable to your business or rental real estate, consider deducting them there instead of as miscellaneous itemized expenses.

Audit alert. The IRS believes that many business and rental property owners are improperly shifting miscellaneous itemized expenses to other parts of the tax return. The expense must truly be ordinary and necessary for your business or rental property for the reclassification to be upheld, and the primary purpose of the expenditure must be to help in the business. Expect an IRS auditor to examine this issue if you are audited and have high deductions under Schedule C or Schedule E for expenses that could arguably belong on Schedule A.

Investment Expenses

You increase after-tax investment profits by deducting some of your investment expenses. Here are some ways to increase those deductions.

Investing as a Business

The benefits of treating investing as a business are that you avoid the 2 percent floor on miscellaneous expenses, are able to make pension contributions based on your investment income and gains, and might be able to deduct for a home office and other expenses. You might even be able to deduct a portion of your health insurance premiums, or hire your spouse and deduct health insurance coverage for him or her.

Unfortunately, the IRS and the U.S. Tax Court believe that investing generally is not a business. To be in the business of investing, the court says you must make transactions often enough to be considered a trader rather than an investor. You probably must trade at least several times a week—though the minimum frequency of trades has not been made clear. And you must be making trades to earn short-term profits, not to earn long-term capital gains. In addition, your portfolio must be sufficiently large that managing it could be considered a business.

Pay Your Spouse to Manage Finances

You can deduct as miscellaneous itemized expenses any salaries, fees, and other expenses that you pay to produce or preserve wealth. The deductions are allowed even if the salary is paid to a relative—including your spouse.

The IRS has approved deducting payments to a spouse to manage the family investments if the spouse does real work, makes the decisions, and the wages are reasonable for the work done. With real-estate properties, these facts are fairly easy to establish. The spouse can collect rents, inspect the properties, make or arrange for repairs, and screen tenants (Revenue Ruling 74-209). With other investments, it is harder to prove the essential facts. At a minimum, the spouse making the payments must not be involved in the investment decisions. In addition, the investments probably should not be held in joint accounts or in the name of the spouse being paid to manage them.

Tax wise money strategy. An alternative strategy, which is easier to get the IRS to accept, is to pay your spouse to keep your books and records. This would not be a full-time job unless you are very wealthy.

In addition to providing tax deductions, paying a spouse allows that spouse to establish an IRA and make contributions, because that spouse now has earned income. But keep in mind that you either have to treat the spouse as an employee and make payroll and withholding tax payments, or the spouse being paid has to report the income as a self-employed person on Schedule C, which means paying the self-employment tax.

Employment Expenses

Deductible employment expenses are any expenditures that are ordinary and necessary for doing your job. The same test applies to expenditures by a business or self-employed person. A difference is that a business or proprietor is not subject to the 2 percent floor. Because of the 2 percent floor, employees should prefer an employer reimbursement plan to a deduction.

In addition, an employment expense is not deductible if it was reimbursed or reimbursable by the employer. The employer must specifically refuse to reimburse or have a policy of not reimbursing for the employee to get a deduction. When you choose not to seek a reimbursement, the expenses are not deductible on your return.

Travel Expenses

The general rule is that when the primary purpose of a trip is business, all associated expenses are deductible. But there are many special rules that you have to follow to be sure of maximizing deductions.

Commuting Expenses

Commuting to and from work is not considered business travel and is not deductible. But there are deductible trips that look a lot like commuting. Here are some examples.

Home office. If your principal place of business is a home office, then travel from that office to another location for business reasons is deductible business mileage. Travel to and from a client's office for a meeting is deductible, as is a trip to buy office supplies or to the post office to pick up or send business mail.

Temporary assignments. If you have a temporary assignment out of town, travel and all other costs related to being out of town are deductible. Deductible business mileage includes trips from your lodging to the assignment.

When the temporary out-of-town assignment is close enough for you to be able to stay in your principal residence each night and commute from there to the work assignment, the daily commute is deductible. Because of these benefits the IRS establishes a few roadblocks to reduce temporary out-of-town deductions.

Out of town. Your regular business location—your "tax home," in the IRS's language—is the metropolitan area in which your office or business is located. So if your temporary assignment is in a different but nearby metropolitan area, you are considered to be out of town on business and can deduct the costs involved. But if you have a temporary assignment across town, you are not out of town for business.

Temporary. If the assignment is permanent or indefinite, you cannot deduct any travel costs. But if it is temporary, all the costs are deductible. After 1993, a temporary assignment is one that lasts for no more than one year. If an assignment is scheduled to last more than a year or in fact lasts more than a year, the assignment is not temporary and you cannot deduct your expenses as out-of-town travel.

Two jobs. When you have two jobs, the cost of traveling between your home and either of the jobs is *not* deductible. But the cost of traveling from one job directly to the other *is* deductible. So it pays not to stop off at home between jobs. Instead, go directly from the first job to the second job.

Appointments. Deductible mileage includes travel from your regular office to business appointments outside the office, and travel from an appointment to your office.

Tax wise money strategy. If an appointment lies on the route from the office to your home, schedule the appointment late in the day. Then after the appointment you can go home instead of back to the office. The miles from your office to the appointment are deductible; the miles from the appointment to your home are not deductible. Or you can schedule the appointment first thing in the morning. The mileage from your home to the appointment is not deductible, but the trip after the appointment to your office is deductible.

Amount of auto deductions. When you use a personal car for business travel, you can compute your deduction using either the standard mileage allowance (29 cents per business mile in 1994) or actual expenses. Under the actual expense method you deduct the business portion of depreciation on the auto, oil, gas, repairs, insurance, tires, and taxes.

If you use the actual expense method, you are subject to the complicated rules limiting depreciation deductions on luxury cars (those costing more than $14,200 in 1993). It can take more than fifteen years to depreciate a car under this method.

Tax wise money strategy. The standard mileage rate is unquestionably easier to use. As a general rule, actual expenses often result in a bigger deduction for people who use the auto more than 50 percent of the time for business. But if your business miles substantially exceed ten thousand annually, deductions might be higher with the standard mileage rate. That's because depreciation is built into the standard mileage rate and is not subject to the annual limit imposed under the actual expense method. The first year you get a car you should keep track of all expenses and compute your deduction both ways. Then use the method that produces the higher deduction and stick with it.

Deduct your motor home. Suppose you travel to the same area frequently on business and do not want to stay at a hotel. For example, a doctor frequently worked at a hospital thirty miles from his office, and when he worked at the hospital often was required to stay several days. The doctor decided to take and stay in his $200,000 motor home on these trips and deducted actual costs based on the percentage of total miles driven for business. The Tax Court agreed that the motor home could be deducted as a business travel and lodging expense (*Hoye,* TC Memo 1990-57).

The same policy can apply to a condominium, yacht, or other facility. If you travel to an area regularly on business, the cost of such facilities is a valid business deduction as long as it is not lavish or extravagant under the circumstances. You also must be careful to limit personal use of the facility, because that could reduce or eliminate deductions.

Out-of-Town Travel

When the principal purpose of a trip out of town is business, then virtually all of your expenses from the moment you leave your home or office until you return are deductible. Even personal expenses such as laundry and dry cleaning are deductible. Here are some ways to use that rule to boost deductions and convert some personal expenditures into deductible business expenses.

Saturday night Layover. You can get substantial discounts on airfares and hotel rooms if you stay over a Saturday night. Recognizing this, the IRS ruled that the hotel and meal expenses incurred in staying over an extra Saturday night can be deductible, even if no additional business activities occur during the extra day, if the extended stay results in a net cost saving (Letter Ruling 9237014).

The deductible family vacation. Of course, you cannot deduct the cost of a family vacation. But you can deduct part of the cost if you combine business with pleasure.

When the principal purpose of a trip is for business, then your personal transportation to and from the location is deductible. The transportation for the rest of your family is not deductible. For the business days of the trip, your personal lodging and meals are deductible. The expenses for your family members are not.

Bonus. If you share a hotel room with your spouse, the additional cost attributable to having your spouse in the room is not deductible. But you still deduct the full cost of a single room for the business days. Normally, the additional cost of having a second person in the room is small, so most of the room's cost will be deductible.

Two businesses or jobs and temporary jobs. Deductions can be very high when you establish businesses or jobs in different parts of the country.

Example. A taxpayer was president of a swimming pool construction business in New England and also established a Florida division of the company to acquire breeding horses and develop a racing stable. The Florida division eventually established a swimming pool construction business. The taxpayer ran both divisions, bought a home in Florida, and lived there during the racing season. The taxpayer deducted all the costs of the Florida home plus meals consumed in Florida. His theory was that the Florida business was seasonal, so his travel there was temporary, out-of-town business travel. The Tax Court denied the deductions, but an appeals court said that one home was the taxpayer's permanent home, and the other was temporary. Deductions were allowed for one of the homes (*Andrews*, No. 90-2165, First Circuit, April 24, 1991).

Foreign travel. Business travel outside the United States faces tougher rules. If you do not spend the entire trip on business, then *all* the travel expenses must be prorated into personal and business portions unless you meet *one* of the several tests. The test you are most likely to meet are that you were out of the United States for both business and personal activity days for a total of one week or less, or that less than 25 percent of the time outside the United States was spent on nonbusiness activities.

Business Meals and Entertainment Expenses

To be deductible, a meal or entertainment expense must be either directly connected with or associated with business.

Directly Connected Expenses

An expense is directly connected with business when all of the following conditions are met:

- You expected a business benefit that was more than a general expectation of a benefit at some indefinite future time.
- You were actively engaged in the conduct of business with the person or persons being entertained at that time.
- Business was the principal aspect of the entertainment activity.
- The expenses were incurred for you and people with whom you do business.

Alternative method. Another and easier way to qualify an expense as directly connected with business is for the expense to be incurred in "a clear business setting." A clear business setting is one in which anyone there would know that your intention was to further your business. An example is a hospitality room at a convention in which business products or publicity are displayed or in which there are business discussions.

Associated with Expenses

A meal or entertainment expense that is associated with business is simply one that is incurred immediately before or after a bona fide and substantial business discussion. The discussion must have a clear business purpose, such as obtaining new business or encouraging the continuation of an existing business relationship.

For the meal or entertainment to occur immediately before or after a business discussion, the two events generally must occur on the same day. But that is not always the case.

Example. An out-of-town client arrives late in the business day. You take the client out to dinner. The next day you have a business meeting. The entertainment is considered immediately to precede a substantial business discussion under the circumstances and is associated with business.

Deduction limit. The 1993 tax hike provides that when a meal or entertainment expense is deductible, only 50 percent of the expense actually can be deducted.

Deducting parties and weddings. You can structure events such as parties and weddings so that they qualify as deductible business meal and entertainment expenses. The event must be small enough so that it is practical and realistic to consider it business-related. Inviting a couple dozen people to your home is realistic. Inviting a hundred or more usually is not.

In addition, there must be an existing business relationship or the realistic possibility of establishing one between you and the guests. If you invite thirty people, of whom ten are business prospects and twenty are neighbors or relatives, the party is not likely to qualify as a deductible business expense. But if you do business with or have the realistic expectation of doing business with the vast majority of guests, you are moving into the clearly deductible area.

The guests must realize that business is mixed with the entertainment. You should, of course, try to have individual discussions about business with as many guests as possible. In addition, you should make a speech or have a presentation that makes clear to everyone what your business is and that you are trying to generate more business. Also helpful would be signs, brochures, and product displays.

You also should be able to show either that you do not give many parties or that you give a mix of deductible and nondeductible parties. Finally, you should keep a record of who attended, the specific business prospects you discussed with them, and any business that actually developed from the event.

Audit alert. Big deductions for meal and entertainment expenses can trigger an audit. You need to be prepared with an itemized list of your expenses and the receipts to back up the list. When you show that these deductions are legitimate, an auditor is likely to conclude that other items on the return are not worth examining.

Conventions

Deductions for conventions have not been allowed as *investment* expenses since 1986. But deductions for business-related conventions are deductible when your attendance benefits or advances your trade or business (or job) and you actually attend seminars, discussions, workshops, etc. Obtaining videotapes to be viewed at your convenience is not sufficient.

To determine if convention attendance was primarily for business, the IRS examines the amount of time devoted to business at the convention versus the amount devoted to recreation and social activities, and whether a resort or nonresort hotel was the site of the convention.

Tax wise money strategy. Keep as many materials pertaining to the convention as you can: programs, handouts, guides, and manuals. Note in the program which sessions you attended. If the convention hands out an evaluation form, keep a completed copy of your evaluation for your records. Any notes you can make that show a direct relation between information at the conference and your business would be helpful.

Foreign Conventions

A foreign convention is one held outside the "North American area," which generally includes Canada, the United States, and most Caribbean and Central American countries. To deduct expenses for a foreign convention, you must meet the regular convention deduction rules and show that it was as reasonable for the event to be held outside the North American area as within it. The following factors are considered:

- the purpose of the meeting and the activities taking place at it;
- the purpose and activities of the sponsoring organization or group;
- the places of residence of the active members of the sponsoring organization and the locations of other meetings held by the group;
- any other relevant factors.

Cruise Ship Conventions

Cruise ship conventions are perhaps the hardest to deduct, and your deduction is limited to $2,000 per year. Of course, the primary purpose of the trip must be directly related to the active conduct of a trade or business. Also, the cruise ship must be registered in the United States, and all ports of call must be in the United States or its possessions.

In addition, you must attach to your tax return a statement signed by you indicating the total number of the days of the trip (excluding days of transit to and from the port) and the number of hours of each day that you devoted to business. The statement also must contain a program of the scheduled business activities.

Further, you must include another statement, signed by an officer of the group sponsoring the convention, that includes a schedule of the business activities each day and the number of hours you attended those business activities.

The Job Search

Job-hunting expenses are deductible as miscellaneous itemized expenses as long as they are not for your first job. You do not even have to take a new job to deduct the expenses, as long as you were seriously looking. Deductible expenses include reproducing résumés, telephone calls, postage, travel, and agency fees.

In one case, the taxpayer was an administrative secretary whose employer relocated. After a few months, she tired of commuting, quit the job, and searched for one closer to home. The job search was conducted while driving a Cadillac Eldorado. The taxpayer deducted actual expenses, including depreciation, and claimed the car was used 70 percent of the time for job hunting. The Tax Court allowed the deduction.

Tax Planning and Legal Expenses

Professional fees related to your taxes and investment are deductible. Many tasks performed by attorneys, accountants, and other professionals affect your taxes and investments as well as other nondeductible matters. For example, estate planning often involves some estate-tax and income-tax planning, but it also involves much nontax matters such as avoiding probate, seeing that individuals are provided for, and putting assets in trusts to protect the principal. The professional costs related to the latter goals usually are nondeductible personal expenses.

Tax wise money strategy. Lawyers and others professionals should be required to itemize their bills to distinguish tax-deductible fees from nondeductible fees. Make this clear to the professional ahead of time or you will miss out on valuable tax deductions.

The Big Three Deductions

Whether self-employed or an employee, most taxpayers would like to deduct for three major items: home offices, personal computers, and cellular telephones. The basic rules are discussed in the chapter on home-based businesses.

Miscellaneous Itemized Expense Checklist

The following items are deductible as miscellaneous itemized expenses on Schedule A. This includes investment expenses, tax-planning and tax-preparation expenses, employee business expenses, and other expenses for the production or conservation of income. The list is not exhaustive.

Accounting fees, for investors
Administration expenses of an estate
Special clothing, for business purposes
Amortization of premiums on taxable bonds
Attorney's and accountant's fees for tax planning and contesting tax claims
Automobile expenses, unreimbursed when used for business
Baseball player's uniforms
Books and publications for business use by employees
Career counseling
Union dues
Custodial fees for investment accounts
Professional association dues
Education expenses that maintain or improve current job skills
Entertainment expenses for business
Meal expenses for business
Lodging expenses for business
Help in obtaining employment, fees paid
Country club, meals, and entertainment for business
Financial counseling fees, for investments or taxes
Gambling losses
Handicap, impairment-related business expenses

Taxes, cost of determining liability
Income-tax-return preparation
Investment expenses
Résumé preparation
Job search costs
Laundry/dry cleaning while on business travel
Legal expenses, investment- or tax-related
Periodicals for investments or taxes
Income-producing property, expenses for the preservation of
Professional books and periodicals
Removal of barriers to handicapped
Safe deposit boxes for preservation of income-producing property
Gifts and presents for clients and customers up to $25 each
Proxy fight expenses
Tools, with a useful life of one year or less
Supplies used in business but not reimbursed
Local travel expenses from one place of business to another
Uniforms for work
Special clothing for work
Shoes, metal-tipped for work
Advisory fees for investments
Appraisal fees for property donated to charity
Estate planning advice, to the extent that the advice is for estate tax planning
Telephone, long-distance business calls made on home telephone
Investment club expenses, member's share of total
Investment counsel fees

Chapter 14

Maximizing Write-offs from Buying and Owning Your Home

If you know the strategies, you can save substantial tax dollars during each phase of home ownership: buying, owning, and selling the home. This chapter focuses on strategies when buying and owning a home; the next chapter covers tax wise ways to sell a home or tap into home equity.

Home Buyers' Tax Strategies

Each home buying expense could be treated in one of three ways. The expense could be:

- a nondeductible personal expense;
- a currently deductible expense;
- a capital expenditure that is added to the tax basis of the property.

Since a first or second home is a personal use asset, an expense can be deducted only if the tax code specifically allows it.

Tax wise money strategy. Retain all the documents related to buying and moving into your home. Not only will you need these to file the tax return for the year of purchase, you also will need them for years to come—especially when you sell the home. Keep your home buying documents for at least as long as you own the home plus three years. The records have to be kept even longer if you defer gain on the sale of the home by purchasing another home.

The most important document to keep is the "settlement sheet." A standardized national form is used in most localities now, and your attorney should provide you with a copy at settlement.

Deductible Home Buying Expenses

There are four types of home buying expenses that might be deductible: interest, mortgage points, real-estate taxes, and moving expenses.

Mortgage interest. You probably will pay some mortgage interest at the contract closing, unless the closing is on the first or last day of the month. You want to be sure to deduct interest paid at closing. The rules for deducting interest paid at closing are the same as those for deducting qualified home mortgage interest while you own the home, discussed later in this chapter. Money paid for a specific service, such as a loan processing fee or an application fee, is not interest.

Mortgage points. Points essentially are prepaid interest and are deductible only when they meet specific IRS requirements.

Most mortgage lenders charge points as a condition of granting the loan. A "point" is 1 percent of the loan. For example, one point on a $100,000 loan equals $1,000. Points generally reduce the rate of interest charged on the loan. A lender might, for example, reduce the interest rate by 0.25 percent for each point you pay.

For points to be deductible at the time of payment, these requirements must be met:

1. The loan must have been made for the purchase or improvement of a *principal* residence. Points on second homes and investment properties do not qualify.

2. The loan must not be secured by property other than the principal residence.

3. Payment of points must be an established business practice in the geographic area.

4. The amount of points charged must not be higher than the amount usually charged in the area.

5. The points must be computed as a stated percentage of the principal amount of the debt.

6. The amount of the points must be paid directly by you.

The last requirement is satisfied if you pay an amount at closing that is at least equal to the points. That amount can be the down payment, escrow or earnest money deposits, or other funds.

Any points that do not meet all of these requirements still can be deducted, but only in equal amounts over the life of the loan. If you pay back the loan before the original due date, any points that have not been deducted can be deducted when the loan is paid.

Seller-paid points. Sometimes to ensure that a property is sold, a seller helps a cash-strapped buyer by agreeing to pay some or all of the points on the mortgage. In 1994 the IRS announced that seller-paid points *are* deductible by the buyer *and* can be used by the seller to reduce the amount realized from the sale. But the buyer's tax basis in the home is reduced by the amount of points paid by the seller.

Real-estate taxes. Real-estate taxes accrue on a daily basis. So when real estate changes owners during the tax year, the amount of taxes must be apportioned between the buyer and the seller according to the number of days each will own the property during the year. The IRS allows the real-estate-tax deduction on a "days owned" basis regardless of any other arrangement between the buyer and seller regarding actual payment of the taxes.

Capital expenditures. Any other expense you incur to acquire or keep title to a home is a capital expenditure. It is added to your basis in the property and could reduce taxes down the road.

Example. You sell a home for $150,000. Your tax basis in the home is $125,000. Your gain on the sale is the amount realized ($150,000) minus the tax basis ($125,000), or $25,000. But if you do not keep careful track of your tax basis and overlook $5,000 of capital expenditures, the gain on the sale would be $30,000.

Capital expenditures included in the tax basis of the home include the purchase price, legal fees, title costs, brokerage commissions, appraisal fees, title and transfer taxes, recording fees, and other closing costs. Any inspections, surveys, or architectural drawings you had done also are included in the basis.

Nondeductible personal expenses. An expenditure that is not deductible and cannot be added to the basis as a capital expenditure is a nondeductible personal expense. It is treated the same as buying yourself a meal or a new suit. Examples include furniture and other personal items that were included in the transaction but are not part of the house or permanently attached to it.

Homeowners' Tax Strategies

Home ownership expenditures are personal expenses that might be deductible as itemized deductions. The commonly deductible home ownership expenses are:

- qualified residence interest;
- real-estate taxes;
- rental deductions on second homes.

Two traps to avoid. Home ownership expenses are deductible only as itemized deductions. If your total itemized deductions do not exceed the standard deduction amount, you get no tax benefit from the expenditures. In addition, high-income taxpayers have their itemized deductions reduced by 3 percent by the amount that their adjusted gross income exceeds a threshold amount ($111,800 for 1994; $55,900 for married taxpayers filing separately).

Mortgage Interest

Several requirements must be met for mortgage interest expenses to be deductible as qualified mortgage interest.

Residence. The mortgage must be placed on either your principal residence or any second dwelling unit you designate. If you own more than two homes, you can designate whichever home you want to be the second residence, and the designation can change each year.

A dwelling unit is *any* property containing cooking facilities, sleeping space, and toilet facilities, including condominiums, cooperatives, mobile homes, recreational vehicles, travel trailers, and boats.

If you rent out the second residence for any part of the year (as with a vacation home), you must actually use the home personally for at least the greater of either fifteen days or 10 percent of the number of days the home is rented. Otherwise the property will be a rental property, not a residence. If you do not rent the home, there is no personal use requirement.

Security. The mortgage must be filed as a secured claim against the house at the local courthouse or other public records office. When all or part of the loan comes from a family member, the seller, or a retirement fund, borrowers often forget to file the security interest.

Acquisition or home equity. A mortgage must be either ''acquisition indebtedness'' or ''home equity debt'' for the interest to be qualified home mortgage interest.

Acquisition indebtedness is debt that you incurred to acquire, construct, or substantially improve your first or second residence. When an acquisition loan is refinanced, only the amount due from the original debt still is acquisition indebtedness. Any additional debt after the refinancing is home equity debt or some other type of debt.

Home equity debt is any debt, other than acquisition indebtedness, that is secured by your first or second residence and that does not exceed the fair market value of the residence minus the acquisition indebtedness.

Proceeds from home equity debt can be used for any purpose without affecting the interest deduction.

Tax wise money strategy. Suppose you plan to incur debt for a personal expenditure, such as buying a car. Normally the interest on that debt would not be deductible. But if you use the proceeds of a home equity loan to pay for the expenditure, the interest is deductible. By using a home equity loan you turn nondeductible interest into deductible home equity interest.

Tax wise money strategy. It makes sense to use a home equity loan to pay credit card balances or other debts that generate nondeductible interest. You will be able to deduct interest on the home equity loan, while you were not able to deduct interest paid on the credit card. In addition, the home equity loan probably will incur an interest rate that is substantially below the credit card or personal loan rate.

Limit. You can deduct qualified mortgage interest attributable to the first $1 million of acquisition indebtedness and $100,000 of home equity debt. These limits are per taxpayer, not per home, and are cut in half for married taxpayers who file separate returns. Married taxpayers who file jointly are considered one taxpayer, so they do *not* get to double these limits.

Helping Out Others

Interest is deductible only by the person who is legally obligated to pay it, who actually pays it, and only when the interest is legally due.

Example. Your adult son loses his job and needs help meeting the mortgage payments for a few months. You make a couple of the payments. You cannot deduct the interest, because you were not legally obligated to pay it. Your son cannot deduct the interest, because he did not make the payments.

Tax wise money strategy. The parents should make a gift to the son of the amount needed to pay the mortgage. The gift will be tax-free as long as the parents give the son no more than $10,000 each year ($20,000 if a married couple gives jointly). An equal amount of gifts also can be given to the son's spouse. Then the son can pay the mortgage directly and qualify for the deduction.

Refinanced Mortgage Interest

When you refinance a mortgage, whether to get a lower interest rate or to take equity out of the home, be careful to preserve your interest deductions.

Acquisition debt still is considered acquisition debt after it is refinanced—but only up to the amount of the original debt outstanding at the time of the refinancing. If you refinance for more than the outstanding debt, the additional debt is not acquisition debt.

Example. You have a home worth $150,000 with an outstanding original acquisition mortgage of $75,000. You refinance the acquisition mortgage with a new $100,000 mortgage. After the refinancing, you will have acquisition debt of $75,000 and home equity debt of $25,000.

AMT alert. If you are subject to the alternative minimum tax, interest on home equity debt is not deductible. And on a refinanced mortgage, only interest attributable to the outstanding balance of acquisition debt immediately before the refinancing is deductible.

Tax wise money strategy. If you are regularly subject to the AMT, it might make sense to take out the maximum mortgage you can when buying a residence and leave your cash invested elsewhere. In that way your interest is deductible under both the regular tax and the AMT.

Points on refinanced mortgages. Mortgage points are deductible in full only when the loan was used to acquire or improve a principal residence, among other conditions. When the points are paid to refinance a loan or to take out a home equity loan, the points are deducted pro rata over the life of the new mortgage.

Exceptions. Points on a refinanced mortgage are fully deductible in the year paid when the loan proceeds are used for substantial home improvements or when the refinancing loan replaces a home construction loan. But these points must meet all the requirements for deductible points described in the previous section.

Shared Equity Financing

A popular way for parents to help children buy a home is through shared equity financing arrangements (SEFA). The SEFA also is used by real-estate investors to help individuals finance the purchase of residences. Under a SEFA at least two individuals own a home together. One individual has the right to live in the home as a principal residence. The other provides key financing and hopes to deduct most of the expenses.

When a financing arrangement qualifies as a SEFA, each owner is entitled to deduct the mortgage interest and real-estate taxes that each actually pays on the property.

To qualify as a SEFA, each of the co-owners must acquire an undivided interest in the property that is scheduled to last more than fifty years. The interest must be in the entire dwelling unit and in any land to which the dwelling unit is appurtenant. In addition, the owner who resides in the dwelling unit must pay "fair rental" to the other owner. This rent is not deductible.

Tax wise money strategy. Shared equity financing is a tax wise way for a parent to help a child buy a home. Under a SEFA, the parent can receive some tax benefits for the payments made to help the child. In addition, a SEFA allows a lot of flexibility, so the terms can be arranged so that the owner with the higher or highest tax rate gets most of the tax breaks.

Real-Estate Taxes

There is no dollar limit on the amount of real-estate taxes you can deduct, no limit on the number of homes for which you can deduct the taxes, and no floor you have to exceed to take a deduction—except that real-estate taxes are deducted only if you itemize deductions. In addition, a real-estate tax frequently can be deducted in the year it actually is paid. So you can deduct some prepaid real-estate taxes if your local tax authority does not put prepayments in a deposit or escrow account.

Tax wise money strategy. In December you decide that an extra tax deduction is needed. So you make the next real-estate tax payment, though the money is not due until the next year. You can deduct the real-estate tax in the year paid. But if you make more than the next payment, the IRS is likely to deny your deduction.

Tax trap. Not all payments you make to the local government qualify as deductible real-estate taxes, and the local government will not make this clear when imposing or collecting the tax. A deductible real-estate tax is one levied for the general welfare, not for specific services or for a particular area. It is not unusual for homeowners in a defined area to pay a "special assessment" for sidewalks, streetlights, or other local improvements. This is not a deductible real-estate tax, since it is not for the general welfare. In addition, any fee that is specifically for a service such as trash collection is not a deductible real-estate tax. Homeowners' association fees or dues also are not deductible real-estate taxes.

Vacation and Second-Home Write-offs

When you own a second home, there are three possible tax treatments of your expenses for owning and maintaining the home. You essentially can choose the tax treatment you want by controlling your personal use and the amount of rental activity for the property.

All personal use. When you don't rent the property, you simply treat it as a second residence. The mortgage interest and real-estate taxes are itemized deductions, and nothing else is deductible. In addition, you can rent the property for up to fourteen days during the year without having to report the rental income or pay taxes on it.

All rental use. You also could rent the property and make limited personal use of it, so it is considered a rental property. Limited personal use means no more than the greater of fourteen days or 10 percent of the total number of days it is rented. Then rental income is offset by all the expenses of owning and maintaining the house, including depreciation. The income and expenses are reported on Schedule E of the tax return. Any losses you incur on the home are limited by the passive activity rules, discussed in the chapter on tax shelters.

Mixed personal and rental use. The rules are more complicated when you make more than limited personal use of the home and rent it for more than fourteen days. Then expenses must be allocated between personal and rental use, and your rental deductions are limited to no more than rental income.

Allocating expenses. Expenses must be allocated between personal and rental use in proportion to the number of days that the property was used for each purpose. For example, if the property's use was 50 percent personal and 50 percent rental, then 50 percent of each expense item is personal and 50 percent is rental. For most expenses, the proportion is the ratio of days the property was rented during the year to the total number of days the property was in use during the year.

But there is controversy regarding the allocation for mortgage interest and taxes. The IRS says that the correct formula is the same as for the other expenses: total number of days rented to total number of days in use. But the Tax Court says that the correct ratio for those expenses is the number of days rented to the number of days in the year. Right now you can choose the method that is more favorable to you, but be prepared to argue with the IRS about it during an audit.

To determine the expense deduction limit, you first subtract from rental income the rental share of mortgage interest and taxes. This has the effect of limiting your deductions for other expenses, because mortgage interest and taxes are deductible as personal expenses anyway. Only the income that remains after subtracting interest and taxes can be offset by other expenses. Any excess deductions can be carried forward, to be used in future years when there might be enough income to offset them.

Personal use days. Keep a log of how the house is used each day. Any day that you, a member of your family, or someone you know is using the home without paying the full rent is a personal use day. But a day is not considered a personal use day when the primary reason for your being there is to work on the home. For example, you could spend most of a regular workday cleaning up the house, getting it ready for the rental season, or making necessary repairs and maintenance. Then you can spend part of the afternoon and evening making personal use of the house. This would not be considered a personal use day because you were there primarily for business and spent most of the day working on the house.

Tax wise money strategy. Many taxpayers find it advantageous not to use their vacation homes as rental tax shelters. They find that the deductions simply are not worth the effort of limiting personal use and keeping logs of how the property is used. Instead, these taxpayers make personal use of the home, lend it to friends, and deduct the mortgage interest and real-estate taxes as itemized deductions.

Chapter 15

Making the Most of Home Equity

When you sell a home, you are likely to have a capital gain. And that capital gain should be taxable. But two provisions can protect the gain from taxes:

- Taxes can be deferred if a new principal residence of equal or greater value is purchased within two years.
- Up to $125,000 of gain can be permanently excluded from income if you are at least age fifty-five at the time of the sale.

The two special tax advantages are available only for the sale of your principal residence. Sales of vacation homes and second homes do not qualify.

This chapter explains how to qualify for and use these two provisions to reduce taxes on home sales. In addition, you will learn tax wise ways in which these and other provisions let you tap home equity.

Home Sale Basics

You have to compute the capital gain on your home sale just as you do for the sale of any other capital asset. You take the "amount realized" on the sale, subtract your "basis," and the remainder is your gain.

Amount Realized
The amount realized begins with the total of:

- cash received;
- the fair market value of any property received;
- the outstanding balance of any mortgage or other debt assumed by the buyer, even if it was a nonrecourse mortgage.

Then you subtract your selling expenses, including broker's fees and commissions, title fees, attorney's fees, and other expenses you incur to make the sale.

Basis

Your basis is essentially your investment in the home. For most taxpayers, it is the original purchase price plus additional costs incurred to acquire title that were not deducted: attorney's fees, title insurance, survey fees, transfer taxes, broker's commission, and similar costs. You can find all of these costs listed on your original settlement sheet.

Your basis is increased by the cost of any capital improvements you made to the property. While capital improvements are added to the basis, repairs are not. A repair is an expenditure that is ordinary and necessary to keep a property in good working order or to maintain its value and usefulness. A capital improvement is an expenditure that increases the value of a property or its useful life. An example of the distinction is that fixing a hole in a roof is a repair, but replacing a roof is a capital improvement.

Other adjustments. You might incur other expenses that are added to the basis. For example, any costs you incur to defend the property's title are added to the basis.

Tax wise money strategy. Keep all records pertaining to the purchase and improvement of your home. You will need these to determine the gain or loss when the home is sold. If you elect to defer gain on the sale, continue holding the records until at least three years after you eventually pay taxes or elect to use the $125,000 exclusion.

Computing the Gain

The difference between the amount realized on the sale and the basis is your gain or loss on the home.

Example. You purchased a home ten years ago for $100,000, including expenses of the purchase. The current mortgage is $60,000, and over the years you added a deck at a cost of $5,000. You sell the home for $150,000. The buyer pays you $90,000 in cash and assumes the $60,000 mortgage. Your selling expenses are a $7,000 broker's commission and $500 in attorney's fees. Here's your gain:

Sale price		$150,000
Less commission	$7,000	
Attorney's fees	500	
		(7,500)
Amount Realized		142,500
Basis		
Original cost	$100,000	
Improvements	5,000	
Adjusted basis		(105,000)
Gain realized on sale		$37,500

Deferring Gain from the Sale

The tax law lets you defer, or roll over, gain from a home sale if you meet several conditions. To defer the gain you must:

- purchase a replacement home for a price equal to at least the "adjusted sales price" of the old home;
- purchase the replacement home within the required time period;
- use both the old and the new homes as a principal residence;
- avoid making multiple sales within a two-year period.

There is no limit to the number of rollovers you can use during your lifetime. You might permanently avoid taxes on all your home sales in one of two ways. One way is to continue owning a home with deferred gain until your death. The other is to defer gain until you qualify for the $125,000 exclusion of gain.

You do not have to purchase an existing home to defer gain. The deferral is allowed when you purchase, construct, or *partially or totally reconstruct* a home. So all the costs of constructing a new home or reconstructing your current residence are treated the same as the purchase price of a new residence. But to qualify, construction expenses must be incurred within two years of the sale of the old residence.

Not an option. If you meet all the requirements, you must defer gain. So if you do not want to defer the gain (you might have a lot of unused capital losses that could shelter the gain), be sure to do something that disqualifies you from the deferral.

Adjusted Sales Price

To defer gain you must buy a new residence that has a purchase price at least equal to the adjusted sales price of the old residence. The adjusted sales price is the amount realized on the sale minus selling expenses, including fixing-up expenses.

Fixing-up expenses. Work that might be done before a home is sold includes painting, landscaping, and other cosmetic work. Usually these expenses are repairs rather than capital improvements, so they cannot be deducted from your income or added to the basis of the old property. But if they meet the following requirements, the fixing-up expenses can be subtracted from the amount realized when computing your deferred gain:

1. *Ninety-day period.* The work is performed within a ninety-day period, ending on the day on which the contract to sell the old residence was signed.

2. *Thirty-day payment.* You must pay for the fixing-up expenses within thirty days after the old residence is sold. In addition, you deduct only out-of-pocket expenses, not the value of your labor or time.

3. *Not deductible.* The fixing-up expenses must be personal expenses that are not otherwise deductible on your tax return.

4. *Repairs, not improvements.* The expenditures must be for ordinary and necessary repairs, not for capital improvements that increase the value of the home or extend its useful life.

Figuring the Deferred Amount
When the adjusted sales price of the old residence is greater than the purchase price of the new home, the difference is taxable.

Example. You are selling a home with a sales price of $160,000 and qualified fixing-up expenses of $5,000. Your broker's commission, attorney's fee, and other selling expenses are $8,000. That makes the adjusted sales price of the home $147,000. To defer all the gain on the sale of your home, the new home you acquire must have a purchase price to you of at least $147,000. If you buy a new home for $140,000, you pay taxes on $7,000 of gain in the year of the sale and defer the remainder of the gain.

Time Period
You must buy the replacement residence within a period ranging from two years before to two years after you sell the old home. The time period is measured from the date the title to the old home legally passes (usually the closing) or when the benefits and burdens of ownership pass as a matter of fact, whichever occurs first.

You not only have to purchase the new home, you also have to move into it and establish it as your principal residence within the time period. The rule on this is very strict. Moving some personal items and furniture, or even all your personal items and furniture, into the new home is not enough. It must be established as your new principal residence.

The IRS and the Tax Court take the position that they cannot make any exceptions other than those in the tax code, regardless of how sympathetic the hardship case is. Taxpayers have been denied deferral of gain in cases of serious illnesses and when the seller of the new residence breached the contract or delayed the closing. In one case, an extension was not allowed, though the new house burned down before the taxpayer could occupy it.

There are a few exceptions set out in the tax code:

- Military service personnel have the time period suspended when they are on active duty, but only for a maximum of four years from the date of the sale.
- Military service personnel who are stationed out of the country also get a special deferral rule.
- When one spouse dies after the old home is sold but before the new residence can be established, the deferral will be allowed to the surviving spouse even if the old the home was owned jointly or was in the deceased spouse's name.
- When a taxpayer moves outside the United States, the time period is suspended, but the new home must be purchased within four years of the sale of the old home. **Note:** The purchase of a foreign residence qualifies for rollover of the gain.

Tax wise money strategy. Be sure to establish the new home as your principal residence within the appropriate time. If the home is under construction, move into whatever portion of the home is livable while the rest of the work is completed.

Tax wise money strategy. Suppose you bought and moved into a new home but are having trouble selling the old home. It looks like the old home will be sold more than two years after you purchased the new home. You can beat the deadline by selling the old home to a relative, as long as it is a real sale. Another option that is becoming more common is to sell the home to your employer.

Principal Residence

Generally any dwelling can qualify as a principal residence if it has sleeping quarters, kitchen facilities, and a toilet. This includes condominiums, cooperatives, boats, house trailers, and mobile homes. You can move from a cooperative to a detached home or vice versa and qualify for the deferral, for example.

If you have multiple homes, the one where you spend the most time is probably your principal residence. If there is some question, the IRS will examine the address on your voter registration, driver's license, vehicle registrations, tax returns, and other official documents. The place where you keep most of your personal effects also is probably your principal residence.

Basis of the New Residence

To compute the basis of the new residence, you first compute its basis in the usual way. Take the purchase price of the residence and add the costs of acquiring title such as commissions, lawyer's fees, title costs, and transfer taxes. Then subtract gain deferred from the previous residence.

You continue this process each time you deferr gain from the sale of a residence.

Multiple Rollovers

Gain can be deferred only once in a two-year period for most taxpayers. If you have multiple sales within two years, then the last residence purchased within the two years is considered the replacement residence for the first residence sold within the two years. Any gain on residences bought and sold in between will be taxable. There is an exception if the moves within the two years are job-related. A job-related move is when the sale was connected with your beginning work or self-employment in a new principal place of work. You also must satisfy the distance and time requirements for the moving expense deduction.

Special Situations

Married couples. A married couple is one taxpayer for purposes of deferring gain. That avoids problems that might occur when each spouse's ownership of the old and new residences are not exactly the same.

Divorced and separated couples. For a couple getting divorced or separated, the situation is very tricky. When the old residence is jointly held and the couple divorces, then each spouse is treated as owning a half share of the old residence. Within the replacement period each spouse must purchase a new residence that costs enough to defer half the gain.

If one spouse does not buy a replacement residence and qualify for deferral, then that spouse will be taxed on his or her share of the old residence. But each spouse will be liable for that tax if the couple filed a joint return in the year of the sale. Therefore the potential liability for such a tax should be negotiated before the divorce is final.

Singles getting married. If each prospective spouse owns a home when they get married, they can sell the old homes and defer gain by purchasing a new residence together. To defer tax, the purchase price of the new residence must be greater than the combined adjusted sales price of the two old residences, and each spouse's adjusted sales price of his or her old residence must be no more than his or her proportionate share of the new residence in order to defer the entire gain of each spouse.

There will be a tax to a spouse to the extent that the adjusted sales price of his or her old residence exceeds his or her share of the new residence.

If each spouse owns a home and if the couple decides to sell one home and move into the other, then the gain on the home sold will be fully taxable. The gain might be deferred if the spouse who sold the home purchases an interest in the other spouse's home, the cost of which exceeds the adjusted sales price of the old residence. But then the other spouse has sold an interest in the home without rolling it over into a new residence. Any gain will be taxable.

The $125,000 Exclusion

You might never pay capital gains taxes on a personal residence.

After rolling over gain on all the homes purchased and sold during your lifetime, you can sell a principal residence after age fifty-four and exclude from income up to $125,000 of gain from that sale. In addition, the $125,000 exclusion can be combined with the deferral-of-gain provision if you have more than $125,000 of gain.

The are two major requirements to qualify for the $125,000 exclusion, known as the ownership test and the residence test.

Ownership test. You must have owned the home for at least any three of the five consecutive years that immediately precede the sale. The three years do not have to be consecutive.

Residence test. You must have resided in the home as your principal residence for at least any three of the five consecutive years immediately preceding the sale. The three years do not have to be consecutive. The ownership and residence periods do not have to be the same three years. The three-year periods also do not have to be calendar years: Any thirty-six months or any 1,095 days during the five years can be added to show you meet the requirements.

Example. You rent a home, using it as your principal residence, for two years. You buy the home at the beginning of the third year and continue to live in it as your principal residence. At the beginning of the fourth year you move out of the home and rent it to someone else. At the end of year five you sell the home. You qualify for the $125,000 exclusion because you have met the ownership and residence requirements separately. There is no requirement that the home be your principal residence at the time of the sale.

Once in a Lifetime

You get to use the exclusion only once in your lifetime, either by yourself or jointly with a spouse. And there is no possibility that you can use it more than once.

Second- and late-marriage rule. If either spouse used the exclusion previously, while either single or married to another spouse, then neither spouse can use the exclusion during their marriage. If the marriage ends, then the spouse who never used the exclusion before can use it after the marriage.

In addition, only one excluded sale or exchange can be reported on a tax return, whether it is a single or a joint return.

Tax wise money strategy. This presents a special challenge to couples who are contemplating marriage after age fifty-four. If each owns a home that has appreciated substantially, they probably want to sell one of the homes and move into the other. Or they want to sell both homes and move into a third home. If they plan to sell both homes and use the $125,000 exclusion, then the homes should be sold and reported on separate, single returns before the marriage. If they do nothing until they are married, only one $125,000 exclusion for one home is allowed.

Age

You must be at least age fifty-five *on the date of the sale* to qualify for the exclusion. You are considered to be age fifty-five for this purpose on the first moment of the day before your birthday.

Example. Suppose you sell your home on August 1, 1995. You turn fifty-five in September 1995. You do not qualify for the exclusion because you were fifty-four on the date of the sale. You needed to wait until after your birthday to sell the home.

Tax wise money strategy. If you have a buyer, are not yet fifty-five, and cannot delay the transaction, consider leasing the home to the new buyer with an option to buy after you are fifty-five. This might work as long as the lease payments are not considered part of the purchase price of the home. You also want to be sure that the lease does not run so long that you miss the three-year residence requirement.

Business Use of the Home

When you use part of your home as an office that qualifies for the home office deduction or as a rental property, you depreciate part of the cost of the house each year. This gives you a tax break while you are maintaining the office. But when you sell the residence, it could create a problem.

The sale of a residence with a home office or rental unit is treated as the sale of two properties: a business property and a residence. You must separate the basis and sale price of the property into the personal-use portion and the business portion. If 20 percent of the home is used as an office, then 20 percent of the basis and 20 percent of the sales price are treated as the sale of a business property, and you will pay tax on the gain from that portion. If the house is sold at a loss, that part is a deductible loss.

Tax wise money strategy. Avoid taxes on part of your home sale by ensuring that the home office or rental unit does not qualify for a deduction in the year of the sale. Study the home office rules in the next chapter and be sure you do not meet at least one of the requirements for the entire year of the sale.

Combining Tax Breaks

The deferral of gain and the $125,000 exclusion can be used in the same transaction. You use the exclusion first, and any leftover gain is deferred.

Example. You are age fifty-eight, have never used the exclusion before, and your home has a basis of $50,000. You sell it for $200,000, with selling expenses of $5,000 and qualified fixing-up expenses of $4,000. You buy a new residence for $65,000. You lived in the old residence and owned it for fifteen years. Your gain and basis are computed as follows:

Realized and Recognized Gain

Selling price	$200,000
Less selling expenses	(5,000)
Amount realized	195,000
Less basis	(50,000)
Realized gain	145,000

Excluded and Deferred Gain

Realized gain	145,000
Less exclusion	(125,000)
Gain not excluded	20,000
Amount realized	195,000
Less fixing-up expenses	(4,000)
Adjusted sales price	191,000
Less excluded amount	(125,000)
Less new purchase price	(65,000)
Amount of gain recognized	1,000

Basis of New Residence

Gain not excluded	$20,000
Less gain recognized	(1,000)
Gain deferred	19,000
Cost of new residence	65,000
Less gain deferred	(19,000)
Basis of new residence	$46,000

Special Tax Wise Money Strategies

The rules for deferring or excluding gain from the sale of a principal residence can be used creatively or in combination with other provisions of the tax code to provide some excellent tax and financial planning strategies for homeowners. Most of the strategies described here have been approved by the IRS or the courts.

Tax-Exempt Investing

The tax code sometimes prohibits a taxpayer from combining certain tax breaks to maximize tax benefits. The primary example of this is the rule that a taxpayer cannot take interest deductions when the loan proceeds were used to buy tax-exempt debt.

But by doing things in the right order you can get the same effect and still be allowed to deduct the interest.

Example. You sell your home at a gain and defer taxes on the gain. You use part of the cash from the sale to make a down payment on the new residence and borrow the rest of the purchase price with a conventional mortgage. The rest of the actual cash proceeds from the sale then are used to buy tax-exempt debt. The tax-exempt interest payments are used to make mortgage payments, and you deduct the interest paid on the mortgage.

Here's the important point that makes this strategy work: *To defer gain on the sale, you do not have to put the actual cash proceeds from the sale of the old residence into the purchase of the new residence* (IRS Private Letter Ruling 8530024). You only have to buy a home with a purchase price at least equal to the adjusted sale price of the old house.

Middle-Class Estate Plans

A major problem for middle-class individuals is that they frequently are house-rich and cash-poor. The problem most of these taxpayers face is that they would like to make some use of the equity in their homes, but they want to remain in the homes for the rest of their lives. They also probably want the homes to pass on to their children.

Key point. There is nothing in the requirements for the $125,000 exclusion that says you have to move out of the home after selling it.

Tax wise money strategy. Sell the home to your children now, but continue to live there. The deal can be structured in several ways. Your children can buy the home through a traditional mortgage arrangement. In that way you get cash today, and they make mortgage payments to the bank. Or you can finance the sale yourself, so the children make payments to you either for the rest of your life or for a period of years.

There also are several ways to structure your continued occupancy of the home.

You can simply rent from the children in a standard rental arrangement at a fair market rent. In fact, you probably can pay a bit less than fair market rent, because renting to a relative justifies a less-than-market rate, since such tenants are considered more reliable than strangers. The children might be able to treat the property as a rental property and deduct any tax losses up to $25,000 annually if their adjusted gross incomes are less than $100,000.

Or the children can allow you to live in the house rent-free for the rest of your life. If the rental value exceeds more than $10,000 annually per child ($20,000 for married children who give jointly with their spouses), the children might be subject to a gift tax on the rental value.

The result of any of these variations is that you have cash flow from the equity in your home and are continuing to live there. In addition, a valuable asset is transferred to your children without probate, and the home is removed from your estate for federal estate-tax purposes.

Key point. For any of the above scenarios to work, you have to make a bona fide sale of the home to your children and cannot reserve the legal right to live in the property if you want the tax and estate-planning benefits. This means that the children must have the legal right to kick you out if they want to.

Temporary Rental of Your Home

Suppose you live in an area with a slow housing market. You are ready to sell your current home and move, but the market is not cooperating. You decide to rent the home while trying to sell it.

The issues when you rent the home are: Which deductions can you can take while renting the home? How you can treat the gain after the home finally is sold?

The IRS says that you can rent temporarily and not lose the tax-advantaged benefits on the sale, but you cannot take rental deductions for the rental period. An appeals court decision ruled otherwise. According to the court, during the rental period you can take all the tax write-offs that a rental property owner normally takes, and you also can defer gain when the house is sold. The court said that there is nothing in the tax code that expressly prohibits both depreciation deductions and deferral of gain from the sale (*Bolaris,* 776 F2d 1428 [9th Cir. 1985]).

The IRS and the Tax Court disagree with this decision, and the decision applies only to the western states covered by the Ninth Circuit Court of Appeals. Other courts are free to disagree with the decision, and if similar cases arise, the IRS will almost certainly take them to court.

If you try this, you should take steps that make it clear that the house is for sale before it is rented and continues for sale while it is rented. You should sign only short-term leases with the tenants and have lease clauses that allow you to cancel the lease on short notice if a sale is made (a kick-out clause). In addition, the tenants should pay the utilities and upkeep so that, if deductions are later denied, you won't have income that went to pay for these nondeductible expenses.

Declining-value trap. When you convert a home from personal to investment use, the basis for computing depreciation or a capital loss is the lower of your basis in the home and the fair market value on the date of conversion. So if the home has appreciated since you bought it, you depreciate only your cost plus improvements. If it has declined in value, you depreciate based on the lower fair market value rather than your cost. And when you sell, your basis is the same as for depreciation, so you are unlikely to have a deductible capital loss.

Convert a Vacation Home

Let's say you own two homes: a principal residence, and a vacation home to which you might want to retire. The vacation home is old and small and needs a lot of work before it is the type of home where you want to spend the rest of your life.

A solution is to spend money redoing your vacation home. Under the rollover of gain provision, the cost of a replacement residence includes the cost of a "partial or total reconstruction" of a home. If you spend money redoing the vacation home, and if the cost is at least equal to the adjusted sales price of your old residence, you should qualify for deferral of gain from the sale of the old home.

Unfortunately, the tax code and regulations are not very helpful in explaining what amounts to a partial or total reconstruction of a home. But the IRS did issue a private letter ruling on the subject. In the ruling, the taxpayer added 35 percent more square feet to the home, a new roof, more basement space, reconstructed a porch, converted storage space into a living area, and replaced the heating and air conditioning. This was considered a partial reconstruction by the IRS (Letter Ruling 8548027).

Buy a Home with Raw Land

Your principal residence is the dwelling unit plus the land to which it is attached. Sometimes there is a question of how much land is considered attached to the dwelling unit. The IRS has decided to resolve this question by saying that any land that is normally considered part of the tract or package with the home or that is sold with the home is considered part of the principal residence.

Suppose that you own a home surrounded by about thirty-five acres. The home has been your principal residence, and you decide to sell the entire package. Let's say you are selling to a developer who is primarily interested in the land and its development possibilities. That does not affect your tax treatment. You are selling your principal residence, and you can defer the gain or exclude it if you meet all the qualifications for those treatments.

The IRS even has ruled that you do not have to sell all the land and the dwelling unit in a single transaction. In one ruling, the taxpayer owned a home with a large lot. He was selling because of his upcoming divorce, but had trouble finding a buyer. The real-estate agent advised the taxpayer to subdivide the property so that he would be separately offering a vacant lot, and a lot with his house on it. The IRS ruled that the sales of both properties would qualify for the rollover of gain. The taxpayer had to establish the new principal residence within two years from the first sale, and the purchase price of the new residence had to at least equal the combined adjusted sale prices of the two properties sold (Letter Ruling 8817015).

You apparently do not have to have purchased all the land in one transaction in order to use this strategy. After moving into a home, you can buy adjoining land and incorporate it into your original lot through landscaping or other means (Letter Ruling 8940061).

This strategy is especially attractive if you live in or are interested in moving to an area that is in the path of growth. You can buy a home and acreage in an outlying area and make it your principal residence. After the property has appreciated, you can sell it and buy a larger home in a more developed area.

Let Your Corporation Buy Your Retirement Home

This is another strategy that has been approved by the IRS in a private ruling.

It works like this. A couple owned a corporation and a suburban home, which they used as their principal residence. The couple had decided where they wanted to retire and had the corporation buy a piece of land there years in advance. The corporation built a house on the land and rented it for several years. The couple exchanged their residence with the corporation for the house and land.

The corporation had held the original house and land as an investment and continued to hold the couple's former residence as an investment property. Therefore the trade qualified as a like-kind exchange to the corporation, so the corporation does not pay tax at this point. The couple qualifies for deferral of gain. The exchange is treated as though they sold the old home for its fair market value and purchased the new home for its fair market value.

In this case, the values of the two properties were not equal. The corporation's house was worth more than the couple's. The couple could give cash or a note to the corporation to make up the difference, and the corporation would be taxed on that amount of its gain. Or they could do nothing and have the excess treated as a dividend to the couple (Letter Ruling 8646036).

Give Your Home Away

You can benefit from your home equity by giving it to charity. Strategies are described in the chapter on charitable giving.

Chapter 16

The Home-Based Business Tax Guide

There has been a boom in business owners and employees who work at home. These "home workers" naturally are interested in maximizing the tax benefits of working at home. This chapter focuses on tax strategies for the "big three" home-based business expenses:

- home offices;
- personal computers;
- cellular telephones.

To be deductible, these expenses not only must be ordinary and necessary for your business, but also your use of them must pass special tests. This chapter also discusses another key issue for home-based workers: how to prove you are conducting a business, not merely trying to take tax deductions for a hobby or other personal activity.

Home Office Deductions

The deduction for a home office potentially is large. In addition, any deduction for a personal computer hinges on your qualifying for the office deduction.

To deduct the expenses associated with a home office, you must meet three requirements.

Regular, Exclusive Use

The first two requirements are that the home office must be used both *regularly* and *exclusively* for qualified business purposes.

Using an office *regularly* means you must not use the office only occasionally but must use it on a continuing basis. If you use the office at least a couple of days a week, you probably are safe, though the tax law is not clear on how regular use must be.

The meaning of *exclusively* is more clear. You cannot use the office area for *anything* other than business. When you are not in there working, the area should not be in use.

But the home office does not have to be a complete room. You can deduct part of a room as a home office if the office portion of the room is separately identifiable (e.g., if it is marked by partitions or a furniture arrangement) and is used exclusively for business.

Tax wise money strategy. Keep a dated diagram or, better yet, photographs of how the office area is arranged. An IRS auditor probably will never see your office but will ask you to bring or mail in proof that it is used regularly and exclusively for business. A diagram or picture is very good proof.

There are two exceptions to the exclusive-use rule. One exception is for taxpayers who provide day care services in their homes. Another exception is for taxpayers in a retail or wholesale business who use a portion of the home to store inventory.

Qualified Business Use

The third test is the qualified business use test. Your home office must be either:

- your principal place of business;
- a place of business for *meeting or dealing* with patients, clients, or customers in the ordinary course of business;
- used in connection with your business if it is a separate structure that is not attached to your house.

You need only one of these qualified business uses to be allowed the home office deduction.

Principal Location

Taxpayers who work in more than one location—such as consultants, medical professionals, salespeople, and others—might have trouble proving that the home office is the principal business location, because in 1993 the U.S. Supreme Court rewrote the rules.

Your principal place of business is determined by two factors: the relative importance of the work done at each location, and the amount of time spent at each location. Generally, the place at which you do the bulk of the work for which you actually are paid is the principal location. If a review of the relative importance of the work done at each location does not clearly indicate the principal office, then you examine the amount of time spent at each location. The location where you spend the most time usually is the principal place of business.

The Supreme Court case involved a self-employed anesthesiologist who maintained a home office to keep his records, review medical files, and line up appointments. The rest of his time was spent at various hospitals, giving anesthesia. The Court ruled that the home office could not be the principal place of business because the tasks performed there were merely administrative or ministerial. The real work for which he was paid— administering anesthesia—was done at the hospitals.

The IRS Speaks

In early 1994 the IRS issued its interpretation of the new rules, using four examples.

Example. The taxpayer is a self-employed plumber who installs and repairs plumbing in customers' homes and offices. He spends about ten hours a week in his home office talking with customers on the telephone, deciding what supplies to order, and reviewing the books. An employee handles administrative chores at the office full time. Another forty hours per week are spent at customer locations. The IRS says that the home office is *not* the principal place of business, because the goods delivered and services performed at the customer locations are the most important part of the business.

Example. A schoolteacher prepares classes and grades papers and tests at a home office for thirty to thirty-five hours each week. A smaller shared office is available at the school, and the teacher spends about twenty-five hours per week at the school, mostly teaching. The IRS says that the activities performed at the school are the more important ones performed by the teacher, so the home office cannot be the principal place of business.

Example. An author spends thirty to thirty-five hours each week writing in a home office. Another ten to fifteen hours each week are spent at other locations, conducting research, interviewing, meeting with publishers, and promoting published works. The IRS ruled that the essence of the author's work is writing, so the home office is the principal place of business.

Example. A self-employed retailer orders costume jewelry from whole-salers and sells it at craft shows, on consignment, and through mail order. About fifteen hours per week are spent at craft shows and consignment shops, while about twenty-five hours per week are spent at the home office handling mail orders, keeping the books, and ordering supplies. The IRS concluded that the most important work is selling, and that is performed at several locations, so the relative-importance test does not indicate a principal place of business. The time spent at each location is examined, and the home office turns out to be the principal place of business because that is where the majority of time is spent.

Tax wise money strategy. If you work at more than one location, keep a log of the time spent and the tasks performed at each location to show that the most important work is done at your home office and that the work done outside the office is less important, such as presenting your final product, or meeting to go over a few points. Or the log can show that the majority of your working time is spent at the home office.

Meeting Customers and Clients

To satisfy this test, you must meet personally with customers, clients, or patients in person in the home office. Telephone contacts are not sufficient. In addition, meetings must take place regularly. Occasional meetings are not sufficient.

Example. A doctor has an office downtown in which he works three days a week. This is his principal office. But he also maintains an office in his home, at which he meets patients two days a week. The home office should qualify for deductions.

Separate Structure

When your home office is in a building that is a separate structure from your dwelling unit, you do not have to establish it as a principal place of business or a meeting place. The office need only be used regularly and exclusively in connection with your business to qualify for the home office deductions when the office is in a separate structure.

Example. A chief executive officer constructed an office in a separate building at his vacation home site. The Tax Court found that the office was helpful and appropriate to his job, because the executive said he needed to get away from the main downtown office periodically to concentrate on long-term planning. It did not matter that some personal considerations prompted the choice to locate the office at the vacation home site instead of at a separate downtown office. Since the office was in a separate structure and was used in connection with business, it qualified for home office deductions.

A dwelling unit is any structure with sleeping space, kitchen facility, and toilet facilities, and anything ''appurtenant to'' that structure. A carriage house, studio, barn, or detached garage might be a separate structure because it is not attached to a dwelling unit. The example used in the IRS regulations is a florist who has a greenhouse in the backyard and a florist shop in another part of town. The greenhouse qualifies as a separate structure used in connection with the business, so home office deductions are allowed.

The Tax Court ruled that an appurtenant structure is one that is directly related to the dwelling unit. The two do not have to be connected physically, and one does not have to be essentially to the other. So structures that appear to be separate might not be separate under the tax law.

Example. A taxpayer owns a house with a detached building on the same lot. The lot is surrounded by a fence, which encloses the two buildings. Both buildings share the same address, and all tax and utility charges for both structures are received in one common bill. According to the Tax Court, under these circumstances the detached building is considered appurtenant to the residence and is not a separate structure.

Maximizing Your Deduction

After qualifying your home office for deductions, be sure that you take the maximum deductions allowed.

Deductible Expenses

You can deduct as home office expenses the pro rata portion of the expenses of maintaining your home, including real-estate taxes, mortgage interest, utilities, insurance, security systems, and depreciation. But you cannot deduct any part of the cost of the first telephone line into the house.

The portion of each expense that is deductible usually is determined on a square-foot basis. If 20 percent of the square footage of the home is used for the office, you can deduct as home office expenses 20 percent of the expenses of owning and maintaining the home. In one case, a couple demonstrated that their entire basement, garage, and part of the first floor were all used regularly and exclusively for business. They were allowed to write off 75 percent of their home expenses as office expenses. You do not have to use square footage to allocate the expenses; you can use any method that makes sense.

Annual Limit

Your home office deductions are limited to your net income from the business activity before considering home office expenses. In computing the limit, expenses related to the home office must be itemized and deducted from net business income in a certain order.

To compute the limit, you begin with the gross income from the business and subtract the home office portions of expenses that would be deductible even if you did not have a home office (real-estate taxes and mortgage interest). Then you deduct business expenses other than those related to the home office. Finally, home office expenses can be deducted to the extent of the remaining net income.

Example. Max Profits has a home-based business that grossed $50,000. He figures that 20 percent of his home is used for business, and he had mortgage interest expense of $10,000 and real-estaste taxes of $2,000. The business expenses not related to the home total $25,000. Max's limit on home office expense deductions for the year is computed as follows:

Gross income	$50,000
Minus 20 percent of mortgage interest	2,000
Minus 20 percent of real-estate taxes	400
	$47,600
Other business expenses	25,000
Home office deduction limit	22,600

Max can deduct the home office portion of depreciation, utilities, insurance, and other permitted home office expenses up to a total of $22,600.

Any home office expenses that cannot be deducted in a year because of the net income limit can be carried forward indefinitely to future years until you have enough net income from which to deduct them.

Personal Computers

The deduction for a home computer depends on the home office deduction. If the computer is used regularly and exclusively at a regular business establishment, including a qualified home office, then the computer is deductible the same as any other business equipment. You can write it off over five years, or elect under Section 179 to deduct the entire expense up to $17,500 in the year of purchase.

But if you don't have a qualified home office, a home computer is known as "listed property." This means it must pass special tests to be deductible. To use accelerated depreciation or to take the expensing election, the computer must be used more than 50 percent of the time for business. If business use is 50 percent or less, only straight-line depreciation can be used.

Tax wise money strategy. The Section 179 deduction is preferable for most home business owners. You can deduct the entire cost of the computer and its peripherals in the first year and do not have to worry about maintaining a depreciation schedule or remembering the depreciation deduction each year. The Section 179 deduction is limited to your net income from the business or $17,500, whichever is lower.

Expensing trap. If you use the computer more than 50 percent of the time for business in the first year, take the Section 179 election, then fall below the 50 percent business-use level in any of the next four years, you have to recapture part of the Section 179 deduction by including it in gross income in the year the business use falls below 50 percent.

When a home computer is used partly for business and partly for non-business activities, any personal-use portion is not deductible. If you use the computer 70 percent of the time for business and 30 percent for personal activities, you can take only 70 percent of the regular depreciation deduction. **Bonus:** When computing the annual depreciation deduction, any investment use counts as business use. But the investment use does not count as business use when determining if the computer is used more than 50 percent of the time for business.

Convenience of the Employer

An employee must meet an additional requirement to deduct a personal computer used at home. The computer must be for the convenience of the employer.

Under the IRS's rules, you must not be able to perform your job properly without the computer and not have one available at work. It does not matter that you can unquestionably perform your duties better with the computer. It also does not matter that you have difficulty getting time on a computer at work because you must share the computer with other employees.

Cellular Telephones

Cellular phones also are listed property. Again, that means the phone must be used more than 50 percent of the time for business in order to use accelerated depreciation or to take the Section 179 expense election for the cost of the telephone. And you deduct only the business-use portion of the phone's cost.

Tax wise money strategy. Keep a log of the calls made and received on the cellular phone. The IRS is not likely to believe that you simply do not make personal calls on the phone. The auditor will insist that you must have periodically called home to check in and make known when you will be arriving. If it is inconvenient to keep a log year-'round, keep logs for periods of time. If these periods are representative of your use year-'round, this is acceptable proof of your use of the telephone.

As with personal computers, the cellular telephone must be required by the employer and required as a condition of employment for it to be deductible by an employee.

Business or Hobby?

When your home business generates tax losses or you are deducting a lot of expenses that could be considered personal expenses, the IRS argues that you are not conducting a business. It says you are disguising a personal activity as a business for tax purposes.

There are two ways to avoid this IRS attack and ensure that your home business is considered a real business for tax purposes.

Five-Year Rule

The easiest way to beat the IRS attack is to make a profit in at least three of five consecutive years. This puts you under the safe harbor of Section 183, and the IRS cannot challenge your business status unless it says that some of the income was not attributable to the business or that you distorted the accounting to show a profit.

Tax wise money strategy. The amount of the profit does not matter, as long as it is a profit. Consider year-end strategies for shifting income and expenses. To ensure that you have a profit this year, you might put off paying some expenses until January, or try to collect early some revenue that might not be paid until next year. If you already have a loss for this year and cannot avoid it, you can try to rescue next year by paying as many expenses as you can this year. You might also try to shift some income to next year by sending out bills late.

Profit Motive Rule

When the five-year rule does not work, you still can establish that you are running a business. There are many taxpayers who never make a profit in their businesses, yet they are able to satisfy the IRS or the Tax Court that they are running businesses and not trying to deduct personal activities.

You can do this by showing that you are genuinely trying to make a profit. It is not enough, of course, simply to state that you are trying to make a profit. You demonstrate your intent through your actions by running the business in a professional manner. Actions that indicate you are genuinely profit-motivated include:

• the amount of time devoted to the business;

- your expertise in the field;
- seeking advice and help from experts in the field;
- proper maintenance of books and records;
- subscriptions to professional journals;
- attendance at professional conferences;
- memberships in relevant trade organizations;
- existence of a business plan.

The potential list is virtually unlimited. You want to assemble enough information to convince the IRS that you really are trying to make a profit but so far have been unable to.

Chapter 17

Tax Wise Ways to Start and Organize a Business

The small business is the best tax shelter available, and the best way to maximize wealth. Business owners have opportunities that simply aren't available to nonbusiness owners.

But too many business owners are paying more taxes than they should because they don't choose the best form of doing business, start and organize the business properly, and plan business transactions carefully.

With tax wise planning you can split income between you and the business, split income between or among family members, receive tax-free and taxable fringe benefits, invest through your business at a reduced tax cost, and eventually sell at a profit in a tax-advantaged way.

Choosing the Form of Business

Your tax benefits get started when you choose the right form of doing business. The choices are:

- sole proprietorship;
- partnership;
- regular corporation;
- S corporation;
- limited liability company.

Unfortunately, many business owners choose their form of business without real tax planning or by using oversimplified guidelines. Important tax planning opportunities can be lost.

The Most Popular Form of Business

Far and away the most common form of business is the sole proprietorship. Most start-up entrepreneurs believe that getting a corporation or other entity formed is too expensive and complicated, so they become sole proprietors by default.

Advantages

Forming a sole proprietorship is simple. Usually all you have to do is get a local business license, though you also might have to register the trade name with the state corporation commission or other government agency.

Tax returns for the sole proprietor also are fairly simple. You attach a Schedule C to your regular Form 1040, listing the income and expenses of the business, and a Schedule SE, computing the self-employment tax, which is the same as the employer's and employee's shares of the Social Security and Medicare taxes. You might have to attach additional forms for depreciation or other special items.

Since income is reported directly on your tax return, it is taxed only once, at your regular tax rate. If you have a loss and were a material participant in the business as defined in the chapter on tax shelters, the loss is deducted directly against any other income you have.

When sole proprietors hire their children, salaries are deductible as long as real work is done and is reasonable for the wages paid. In addition, when a child is under age eighteen and the business is not incorporated, the wages are exempt from Social Security and Medicare/Medicaid taxes. Each child can earn up to the standard deduction amount tax-free each year ($3,800 in 1994).

Disadvantages

As an unincorporated business owner you are personally liable for all debts and liabilities of the business. If the business goes bankrupt, so might you. As a practical matter, incorporated small business owners often have to assume personal responsibility for most loans and credit extended to their businesses. But if someone is injured on the business premises or sues the business for a personal injury, the owner of an incorporated business might be protected when the sole proprietor would not be.

It can be difficult to buy and sell a proprietorship or pieces of it. If you want to bring in investors or co-owners, you have to form another entity, such as a partnership or corporation. With a proprietorship, you have a collection of assets that can be sold either as a package or separately—and they probably aren't worth much if sold separately.

A proprietor cannot split income with the business, since it is not a separate taxpayer. In addition, the tax law limits the tax-free benefits available to owner-employees of unincorporated businesses. So the proprietor cannot pay personal expenses through the business with tax-free income the way a corporate owner can. Estate planning also is more difficult for the proprietor than for the owner of one of the other business forms.

Using a Partnership

Partnerships can be used in any type of business, not just tax shelters.

There are two types of partnerships: the general partnership and the limited partnership. In the general partnership, all partners are general partners, usually are able to participate in management decisions, and have unlimited personal liability for the debts and obligations of the partnership. In a limited partnership, there are one or more general partners and one or more limited partners. The limited partners are investors only, or silent partners. The general partner makes business decisions and has unlimited personal liability. The limited partners have little say in how the business is run, and the liability of the limited partners usually is limited to their investments in the partnership plus any debts of the partnership that they assume or guarantee.

The partnership is known as a ''pass-through entity'' for tax purposes. That means that the partnership itself is not taxed, but files a tax return showing its income and deductions for the year and reports each partner's share of those items to both the partners and the IRS. The income and deductions are reported on the returns of the individual partners.

Advantages. A partnership is easy to form and is very flexible. In most states, a general partnership does not even need a written partnership agreement to be valid (but you should always have a written agreement, especially for tax purposes). Partnership interests are easier to buy and sell than interests in a proprietorship, making it more attractive to investors. Limited partnerships are especially attractive to outside investors.

Since income and expenses pass through to the partners, income is taxed only once, instead of being double-taxed, as with a corporation. And if the partnership has tax losses, these can be deducted on the returns of the individual partners (subject to the passive activity loss limits) and reduce each partner's taxes on other income.

Disadvantages. The bookkeeping and tax reporting for a partnership can get complicated. Even a small, passive limited partner can have the annual tax return preparation fee increase by over $100 because of the additional work required in dealing with Form K-1, which lists each partner's income and expenses.

Limited partners are at an extreme disadvantage. They have virtually no rights under the law and most limited-partnership agreements unless a general partner commits outright fraud. Even reviewing the books is a restricted right, so any fraud by a general partner might not be discovered right away.

Each general partner and the partnership as a whole are liable for any promises and obligations a general partner makes on behalf of the partnership—and also for the negligent acts of each general partner. That is why many law and accounting partners are having financial difficulties these days. Each partner has to pay a share of the judgments rendered against other partners for negligent actions.

Because of the pass-through of income and expenses, tax deferral and income shifting are difficult. In addition, partners who also work as employees of the partnership are not entitled to the same tax-free benefits that a corporate owner-employee is.

Incorporating Your Business

A corporation is a separate legal entity, actually considered a separate "person" under most laws, when it is properly formed under state law. This separate legal status results in a number of advantages and disadvantages.

Advantages. As a separate person, with some exceptions the corporation generally shields the shareholders from personal liability for the debts and obligations of the corporation.

Corporate shares also are the easiest form of business ownership to buy and sell. Minority owners prefer corporations because shareholder rights are more clearly defined and often are broader under state corporate law than the rights of owners of other business entities. These two factors, plus the limited legal liability, make the corporation the vehicle of choice for business owners who are looking to attract investors.

As a separate legal entity, the corporation provides you with a number of tax-saving opportunities. You can take a salary from the corporation and have some of the income taxed to you, while leaving other income in the corporation to be taxed at its rate, which starts at 15 percent and rises to a maximum 34 percent for small businesses. The corporation also gives you the opportunity to lease property to the corporation, hire relatives, and engage in other income-shifting opportunities.

The corporate tax rate schedule for small businesses is as follows:

Taxable Income	Tax Rate
$0–$50,000	15%
$50,000–$75,000	25%
$75,000–$100,000	34%
$100,000–$335,000	39%
$335,000–$10,000,000	34%

Because of the corporation's separate tax rate schedule, when the business's income exceeds what you need for your standard of living, it makes sense to take an appropriate salary and benefits (deductible from corporate income) and have all or most of the "excess income" retained in the corporation to be taxed only once and at lower rates than yours. A corporation can accumulate income up to an aggregate of $250,000 of profits plus funds accumulated for reasonable business purposes. After that, an accumulated earnings tax is imposed on undistributed profits.

The corporate owner who also is an employee of the corporation can, for the most part, receive the same tax-free benefits that are available to other employees of the business. For example, corporate owners receive tax-free health benefits, while other owners must include business-paid health benefits in gross income. Corporate owners can receive the whole range of benefits tax-free to them and deductible from corporate income. Many corporate owners pay enough salary and tax-free benefits that the corporation's taxable income is zero, so the income is taxed only once.

Until the 1980s a major reason to incorporate was to get a better pension plan than was available to other business owners. But during the 1980s the pension plan rules were changed so the main difference now is that many corporate owner-employees can borrow from their plans, while unincorporated owner-employees cannot.

The corporation also can be a good vehicle for making investments. In addition to benefiting from lower tax rates, a corporation can exclude from income 70 percent of the dividends it receives on stock of other, unrelated corporations. Also, the passive loss rules that limit tax shelter deductions do not apply to many corporations.

The corporation also can make estate planning easier for an owner who wants to retain the business and pass it on to his or her children over time.

The corporation also gives you the unique ability to get something for nothing. Suppose you form a business and it fails. In most cases, your investment in the business is a capital asset, and your capital loss is deductible up to your capital gains for the year plus $3,000. Any unused loss is carried forward to future years.

But when you form a corporation you can make a "Section 1244 election" in the corporate minutes. Then any loss you incur from a failure of the corporation is an ordinary loss deductible against all your income in the year of the loss.

Alert for professionals. Many of the tax benefits of a corporation are not available to professionals. A "personal service corporation" is taxed at a flat rate of 34 percent, so you get little benefit from accumulating income in the corporation or shifting taxable income to the corporation. In addition, personal service corporations do not qualify for the corporate exception to the passive loss rules. Affected professionals include doctors, dentists, lawyers, accountants, architects, engineers, and consultants.

Disadvantages. It costs additional money to set up and maintain a corporation. Though in most states it is easy to set up a corporation yourself, most people do not know how to go about it and end up paying a lawyer $500 or more. The corporation needs bylaws, regular meetings, minutes of the meetings, and documents for all transactions between owners and the corporation. You also must pay an annual fee and file an annual report with the state corporation commission or other entity and file separate returns.

Also, when you want to take out money beyond your salary and benefits, it will be taxed twice—once when the corporation reports its taxable income, and again as a dividend on your return.

In addition, the IRS targets small corporations for audits because it believes small-corporation owners do not jump through all the hoops. A corporation that does not have all its paperwork in order or does not receive good tax advice on structuring a transaction is especially vulnerable to attack from the IRS.

A regular corporation also is subject to some tax penalties that do not apply to other businesses. A personal holding company tax is imposed on a corporation that earns most of its income from investments and does not distribute that income to shareholders. Also, a corporation might not be considered a corporation for tax purposes if the IRS decides it is a "sham corporation." Corporate owner-employees have to justify their salaries as being reasonable, or the IRS will decide that part of the salary is really a dividend. In addition, corporations that accumulate income beyond $250,000 plus the reasonable needs of the business can be hit with an accumulated-earnings tax.

Winding down the corporation also can be expensive. When a corporate owner decides to sell the assets and liquidate the business, there might be a double tax. One tax is imposed when the corporation sells the assets, another when the shareholder receives the liquidation distributions.

Choosing the S Corporation

The S corporation is a special creature of the tax law, and all the differences between the S corporation and a regular corporation are tax differences. Under state corporate law, an S corporation and a regular corporation are treated the same.

The S corporation, also known as a small-business corporation, is a corporation formed under state law, with no more than thirty-five shareholders, only one class of stock, and that meets other requirements. An election to be an S corporation must be filed with the IRS.

The S corporation pays no taxes in most cases. Income and expenses are reported to the IRS, and each shareholder gets a Form K-1, on which his or her share of the income and expenses is listed. The shareholders report the K-1 items on their own returns.

The S corporation is sometimes called a corporation that is taxed like a partnership, but that is not accurate because there are tax differences between the S corporation and a partnership. It really is a hybrid, a corporation under regular law that has a separate tax structure. The S corporation might be taxed when it sells some of its assets. Another major difference between an S corporation and a partnership is how the owner's tax basis is computed. In each case, an owner can deduct losses on his or her own tax return only to the extent of the owner's tax basis in the business. But in a partnership, a partner's basis includes his or her share of the partnership's debts. An S corporation owner's basis, however, does not include a share of corporate debt. It includes only money the shareholder has given or loaned to the corporation, and a share of the corporate debts personally guaranteed by the shareholder.

Advantages. S corporations became very popular after the Tax Reform Act of 1986 when for the first time the top individual tax rate (28 percent) was less than the top corporate rate (34 percent). Owners of successful businesses found they could save a great deal of money simply by having corporate income taxed to them on their individual returns instead of taxed to the corporation.

The top individual rate no longer is less than the top corporate rate, but there still are advantages to an S corporation. S corporation income is taxed only once. If you are receiving a maximum salary and benefits and want to take more money out of the business, this is important.

When the corporation is experiencing losses, the owners might want to have an S corporation so they can deduct the losses on their individual returns instead of having them locked up in the corporation.

In addition, most of the time an S corporation and its owner pay only one tax after selling the assets and liquidating the corporation. With a regular corporation, both the corporation and the shareholder would be taxed. But the double tax is not avoided if the corporation elected S status in the past ten years and had "built-in gains" in its assets when it made the S election.

An S corporation also is not subject to the corporate minimum tax, personal holding company tax, and accumulated earnings tax, and it might be allowed to use the cash method of accounting when a regular corporation cannot.

Disadvantages. The big disadvantage of the S corporation is that corporate owner-employees do not get many of the tax-free benefits as do regular employees or as owner-employees of regular corporations. Under the tax law, any employee who owns 2 percent or more of an S corporation or a partnership cannot take full advantage of tax-free benefits.

Since the maximum individual tax rate now is 39.6 percent and the basic corporate rate is 34 percent, at some income levels there is an incentive to have a regular corporation so that some of the business income is taxed to the corporation at its rate instead of to the shareholder. But you don't want a regular corporation if you plan to take all or most of the income out of the corporation each year. You want an S corporation so the income is taxed only once.

There are limits on the type and number of S corporation shareholders. Corporations and most trusts cannot be S corporation shareholders. Also, it is easy for an S corporation to lose its S status inadvertently, because of a failure to comply with all the S corporation requirements. S corporation managers need to consult a tax adviser before making ownership or business changes.

A partnership has an advantage over an S corporation in that the partners can, within limits, decide how to allocate income and deductions between or among themselves. The allocations do not have to be the same as the ownership interests. Partners with substantial outside income can be allocated a greater share of the losses, and partners in low tax brackets can be allocated more of the income. In an S corporation, the income and expenses pass through to the shareholders in direct proportion to the ownership interests.

Not all states recognize the S corporation. You might find yourself in th position of filing a regular corporation tax return and paying corporate income taxes in your state while being taxed as an S corporation by the federal government.

Tax wise money strategy. You probably want to avoid an S corporation when you would end up in the highest individual tax bracket as an S corporation shareholder, plan to reinvest most of the corporation's earnings to fund its growth, and the corporation does not have appreciated assets that would be subject to double taxation if sold by the corporation. Otherwise you should consider the S corporation when corporate taxable income after your salary and benefits is in the $100,000 to $150,000 range.

New Item on the Menu

The limited-liability company (LLC) is very new to business planning. These entities are intended to give the limited-liability protection of corporations but be taxed as partnerships by the IRS. The first limited-liability company law was enacted in Wyoming in 1977, but the entity was dormant until the IRS finally ruled in 1988 that the LLC would be taxed as a partnership. Since then almost every state has adopted an LLC law.

Advantages. The idea of an LLC is that you get the benefits of an S corporation (limited liability, no double taxation) without most of the disadvantages. The LLC also is useful if you want a foreign person to be an owner; a corporation cannot elect S status if all shareholders are not U.S. persons, but LLC owners can be of any nationality.

Disadvantages. This is a new area of the law, so you cannot be sure of the answers to many questions involving shareholder disputes, liability of owners to outside parties, and other basic questions. If you form an LLC, yours could be a test case someday. If you do business in more than one state, you probably should not use an LLC, because the state laws vary and there are too many unanswered questions.

An LLC also can be expensive to form, costing at least as much in legal fees as forming a corporation.

Another potential disadvantage is that when one owner leaves the LLC, all owners must formally agree to keep the LLC in existence. This could be a problem if there are many owners or some disagreements among the owners.

Organizing Your Business

How do you choose a form of doing business?

Most important is to consider the nontax factors first. If you need limited liability and will have more than own owner, you should not have a proprietorship or a general partnership. Also consider the cost, flexibility, attractiveness to investors, and estate planning.

Then make a reasonable forecast of the business's income and expenses for the next year or two.

Example. Max Profits is running a small business as a sole proprietor with no employees. His taxable net income for the year is $50,000, and he expects over the next year or two that the results will be similar. As a proprietor his taxes are:

Federal income tax	$9,060
State income tax	2,000
Self-employment tax	7,650
Total taxes	18,710
After-tax cash	31,290

From this after-tax cash, Max pays his and his family's medical expenses, which totaled $2,000, plus all his other regular living expenses.

Suppose Max incorporates his business and establishes a health plan for the corporation's employees (himself). Max figures that after taxes he needs about $25,000 to $30,000 to maintain his lifestyle. After one year of operating the business through a regular corporation, Max has the following results:

Net corporate business income	$50,000
Less health plan expense	(2,000)
Less Max's salary	(44,000)
Less employer's payroll tax	(3,443)
Corporate taxable income	557
Corporate income tax	84
Max's federal income tax	7,380
Max's state income tax	1,760
Max's employment taxes	3,366
Max's after-tax cash	31,494
Total taxes paid	16,033

By incorporating, Max has $2,677 more after-tax cash, pays less in total taxes between him and the corporation, and has his medical expenses paid with pretax dollars.

Tax wise money strategy. Estimate your revenues and expenses for the next few years. Then you or your tax adviser should compute the estimated taxes you would incur under different forms of doing business. Select the form that provides the most after-tax wealth and is consistent with your nontax needs and goals. Do not pay high fees to a tax adviser to give you rules of thumb or guidelines.

As your business changes, the form of business can change. You can move from a proprietor to a corporation to an S corporation over time as the business changes.

Tax wise money strategy. A sole proprietor might not need to incorporate to get tax-free health benefits. An IRS ruling involved a proprietor who hired her spouse to work in the business. The spouse was covered by a written medical reimbursement plan for employees and used it to pay all the medical expenses of the couple and their children. The medical benefits were tax-free income to the couple and were deducted by the proprietor on Schedule C (Private Letter Ruling 9409006).

Tax Wise Incorporating

Most business owners eventually choose to move from a proprietorship to some form of corporation. If you choose that route, you can avoid many estate-planning and double-taxation problems by carefully planning the incorporation. You could make or lose tens of thousands of dollars over the rest of your lifetime because of the steps you take when forming a corporation.

Key point. You do not need to put all the business assets in the corporation.

For example, appreciating assets usually should be kept out of the corporation. Presumably you will sell the assets someday and will want to avoid the double tax on the profits. You can do that only by keeping the assets out of the corporation to start with.

Keeping assets out of the corporation also gives you income-splitting possibilities. You, or your children, can rent valuable assets to the corporation. The corporation will pay rent, which will be deductible from corporate income. You will receive income that might be sheltered by depreciation and interest deductions from the property. This income supplements your salary. If the assets are owned by your children, any net income is taxed at their tax rate instead of yours. This strategy often is used for business real estate.

The Benefits Of Multiple Corporations

Suppose you decide that a regular corporation is the appropriate vehicle for your business. After some years, the business prospers, corporate income grows, and you look for ways to further reduce taxes on the corporation. One way to do that might be to split the corporation into several corporations.

Remember the basic principle of income-splitting. Since tax rates are graduated—meaning that the marginal tax rate rises as taxable income rises—you can reduce taxes simply by splitting the income among several taxpayers. Instead of having one corporation in the 34 percent tax bracket, you can try to have several corporations, each of which is in the 15 percent bracket.

The tax savings can be significant. When your corporation is in the top tax bracket, each additional corporation you can split income with reduces overall income taxes by about $11,750. When compared with having an S corporation, which has its income taxed at the owner's 39.6 percent tax rate, you can save about $18,500 per corporation that stays in the 15 percent tax bracket.

Tax wise money strategy. Multiple corporations can be good for a profitable small business that has up to $2 million in taxable income. The tax savings easily outweigh the costs of maintaining separate corporations and their books and records.

Since multiple corporations are such an effective tax-reduction strategy, Congress has given the IRS a couple of tools to use to limit the use of multiple corporations.

One tool provides that when one corporation owns 80 percent or more of another corporation (parent-subsidiary corporations), they will be treated as one for most tax purposes. The aggregate income of all the related corporations will be taxed as though earned by one corporation.

Under the other provision, when two corporations are each 80 percent or more owned by the same five or fewer persons, and the same five or fewer persons own more than 50 percent of each corporation, then these "brother-sister" corporations will be taxed as one corporation. Again, the benefits of multiple corporations will be lost.

Tax wise money strategy. You can avoid having multiple corporations treated as brother-sister corporations by letting employees own 20 percent or more of each corporation. You also can bring in unrelated outside investors for one corporation, but be sure that those investors do not own interests in the other corporations. These strategies allow you to enjoy the tax benefits of multiple corporations.

When you split a current business into more than one corporation, you must demonstrate nontax reasons for the split. This usually is not a problem unless your business has only one location and there is no logical way to separate different parts of the business.

Tax wise money strategy. When considering an expansion of your business, strongly consider putting the expansion into a separate corporation. This is especially appropriate when the expansion involves either a new line of business or an additional location for the business.

Chapter 18

Taking Cash out of Your Corporation

Corporate income is potentially subject to double taxation: one tax on the corporation, and another tax when the owner withdraws the money as a dividend. Because of that, small corporation owners look for opportunities to take cash out of the corporation in tax wise ways.

Despite recent restrictions and increased costs, qualified retirement plans still are among the best tax wise money strategies for taking cash out of a corporation, and every business should consider them. This chapter discusses the different types of plans and when each is appropriate. It also has a checklist of other tax wise ways to take cash out the corporation that are discussed in other chapters.

There are four types of qualified retirement plans to consider:

- 401(k) plans;
- profit-sharing plans;
- defined-contribution plans;
- defined-benefit plans.

Each of these plans offers four benefits: deductible contributions by the employer, no immediate tax on the employee, tax-deferred compounding of income earned on pension investments, and tax-favored treatment when funds are withdrawn.

Another advantage under most types of pension plans is that employees can borrow from their accounts. When an employee pays the money back with interest, that person essentially is paying interest to himself or herself. Not all employees or retirement plans allow loans. Owners of unincorporated businesses, for example, cannot borrow from Keogh plans. If loans are important to you, check with your tax adviser before selecting a pension plan.

401(k) Plan

This usually is the first qualified retirement plan a small business should consider. The only costs the employer incurs are setting up, maintaining, and administering the plan. The 401(k) allows a small business to give employees a tax-advantaged opportunity when the business cannot afford to make contributions for employees.

In a 401(k) plan, an employee decides how much of his or her salary to defer each year. The salary is withheld from each paycheck and deposited in the employee's 401(k) account. The employee does not pay income taxes on the deferred salary, but the deferred salary is subject to Social Security and Medicare/Medicaid taxes.

The amount each employee can defer has two limits. There is an absolute limit, indexed for inflation, which was $9,240 for 1994. In addition, "top-heavy" rules in the IRS regulations require a minimum percentage of the total deferrals to come from nonhighly paid members of the workforce. If the lower- and middle-level workers do not make enough use of the 401(k) option, the "excess deferrals" of highly paid employees are returned to them.

An employer that can afford to be more generous and that wants to encourage more participation in the 401(k) can match employee deferrals. Employers usually offer to put in $0.50 to $2 for each dollar an employee defers. The employer's matching contribution does not count against the employee's annual absolute contribution limit.

Profit-Sharing Plans

The next plan to consider is the profit-sharing plan. The employer makes all contributions in these plans, but there is *no required annual contribution.* When the business is profitable, the corporation can elect to make a contribution to the plan. In years when cash is tight, no contribution has to be made.

The employer decides how much of a total contribution to make each year, but once that decision is made, the contribution is divided among employee accounts according to a formula set forth in the plan. There is some flexibility, but generally a fixed percentage of an employee's salary is added to his or her account.

Defined-Contribution Plans

In a defined-contribution plan, the employer makes annual contributions equal to a percentage of salary. Unlike a profit-sharing plan, *annual contributions are required* each year once the plan is set up. That is why you want to consider a profit-sharing plan first and set up a defined-contribution plan only after you are confident that the corporation's cash flow has hit a certain minimum level.

There is some room, but not a lot, to give key and highly paid employees larger contributions. For example, a plan can be "integrated" with Social Security so there is one level of contributions for salaries below the maximum Social Security wage base, and another level of contributions for salaries above the wage base. But changes over the past fifteen years reduce the extent to which Social Security integration and other provisions can be used to give highly paid employees extra contributions.

Defined-Benefit Plans

These plans are the most expensive to set up and maintain, but they potentially create the largest tax deductions and the largest account balances over time.

A defined-benefit plan promises an employee a fixed annual or other periodic payment during retirement. An actuary looks at the life expectancy of an employee, the expected earnings of the pension fund, the expected benefit to be paid, and other factors to determine the annual contribution required to fund the future benefit. The expense of having the actuary make these calculations drives up the cost of maintaining the plan each year.

Annual contributions to the defined-benefit plan are required. If the investment return of the pension fund falls below expectations, the contributions might have to increase in the future. On the other hand, if investment returns exceed the estimates, the plan might become "fully funded," which would prohibit future contributions. Again, you do not want to set up one of these plans if you are not comfortable that the business has established a reliable level of cash flow.

Tax wise money strategy. Defined-contribution plans tend to benefit workers under age forty. Projections show that younger employees end up with larger retirement funds under a defined-contribution plan than under a defined-benefit plan. Employees age fifty or over would get the largest benefit from a defined-benefit plan. In between is a gray area that depends on the assumptions you make. Younger business owners should consider defined-contribution plans, and older owners should favor defined-benefit plans.

Tax wise money strategy. Most successful businesses end up with several retirement plans. You start with a 401(k) plan, which costs the firm little money. When the business starts to grow, add a profit-sharing plan, which makes contributions in years when the business can afford it. After the business has a reliable minimum cash flow, you set up a defined-contribution plan or a defined-benefit plan. A good strategy is to determine the amount of money you feel will always be there to make retirement plan contributions even in bad years, and set up a defined-benefit or defined-contribution plan that requires roughly that level of contributions. In good years you can make additional contributions to the profit-sharing plan. This combination of plans means that corporate cash flow will not be crimped by required pension plan contributions in tough years.

Hybrid Plans

The biggest reason that small-business owners give for not setting up retirement plans are nondiscrimination rules. These rules, and the top-heavy rules, prevent small-business owners from getting the bulk of the annual contributions. To many small-business owners, this means that the cost of the plan exceeds the benefits to them.

Under the traditional profit-sharing plan, for example, the corporate contribution to the plan is allocated among participants according to salary. If the profit-sharing contribution is 10 percent of the business's payroll, then each employee's account gets a contribution of 10 percent of his or her salary. But under new IRS regulations, "hybrid" versions of profit-sharing plans can boost benefits to owners. The hybrid plans allow contributions to favor older and long-term employees by taking age and years of service into account when allocating the corporate contribution among plan participants.

Age-Weighted Plan

This plan allows the employer to satisfy the nondiscrimination rules by looking at the expected future benefits under the plan instead of current contributions. That means that larger contributions can be made for older employees (such as owners and executives) because they have less time until retirement. This is not desirable if the owner is not among the oldest employees or if co-owners are not close in age. Otherwise the age-weighted plan might be more attractive than a traditional profit-sharing plan.

Comparability Plan

Under this plan, employees are divided into groups, and employees in each group get the same percentage of their salaries allocated to their accounts. The IRS says that the groupings are valid as long as the projected future benefits for regular employees are at least 70 percent of the projected benefits for owners and highly compensated employees. Since projected future benefits are the yardstick, a comparability plan can be attractive if the owners are on average at least five years older than the average of the rest of the workforce.

These new hybrid plans can allocate a greater percentage of the benefits to owners in many cases. But the annual contributions have to be calculated by actuaries, and this increases the cost of maintaining the plan.

Simplified Employee Plans

Custom pension plans can be expensive, costing $1,000 or more to set up plus that much each year to maintain. Small businesses that cannot afford these costs can choose simplified employee pensions (SEPs), which are essentially super IRAs.

Under the SEP, the employer (or self-employed individual) makes contributions to IRAs established for each employee. The contributions are a fixed percentage of each employee's salary and cannot exceed $15,000 per employee each year. After the money is in the SEP, it is treated the same as any IRA.

A drawback of the SEP is that employees do not get to use one of the lump-sum averaging methods when they withdraw money. They also cannot borrow from the IRA as they can from most other types of retirement plans. The employer must make an SEP contribution for every employee whose salary or wages was more than $325 (indexed for inflation) during the year.

401(k) SEP

SEPs are allowed to add a 401(k) feature to their plans. These plans are subject to the same deferral limits as regular 401(k)s are.

Tax wise money strategy. Because they are not flexible and lack many features of other retirement plans, SEPs should be used only by small businesses with one or two employees. Other businesses should consider the regular pension plans.

Cutting Costs

If you are concerned about the cost of setting up a qualified retirement plan, you can get an affordable plan if you are willing to give up customized features. Most financial institutions—banks, insurance companies, mutual funds—have basic pension plans approved by the IRS. The plans are available for low fees, but, of course, you are expected to keep the plan's assets invested with the financial institution. These off-the-shelf plans usually do not include defined-benefit plans. You need a pension consultant and actuary for those.

Nonqualified Deferred Compensation

Because of the restrictions imposed on qualified retirement plans in recent years, many business owners and highly paid employees feel they cannot save enough for retirement through these plans. For these taxpayers, there are nonqualified deferred-compensation plans.

Nonqualified deferred-compensation plans are discussed in Chapter 10, "Retirement Planning for Late Starters."

A big advantage of a nonqualified deferred-compensation plan to the business owners is that you can cover as many or as few employees as you want. That makes such a plan a very attractive way to keep key employees happy.

A Checklist of Benefits

Pension plans are a big benefit of owning a business. But there are many other tax wise ways to take cash out of the small business, especially a corporation. They are discussed in other parts of this book. Among them:

- Tax-free fringe benefits—these include health insurance, group term life insurance, working condition fringe benefits, no-additional-cost benefits, and others.
- Family income shifting—a corporation gives you many opportunities to hire family members and essentially pay tax-deductible allowances to your spouse, children, and other relatives. The payments are deductible to the corporation and taxed at the tax rates of your children or whoever else receives them.
- Leasing transactions—you or your children can acquire business property and lease it to the business. The lease payments are deductible

by the business, and the income is partly tax-sheltered by depreciation write-offs from the property.

- No-interest loans—you or your family members can benefit by receiving from the corporation loans on which below-market interest or no interest is charged. Even after the changes made by Congress in the 1980s, low-interest loans are very attractive.
- Split-dollar life insurance—the corporation can help you and other employees buy life insurance at very low cost; the only cost to the corporation is the time value of its money.
- Personal living expenses, tax-free.
- Estate planning—an incorporated business gives you a number of flexible options in your estate planning. Using one or more of these strategies allows you to leave more wealth to your heirs.

Chapter 19

Sheltering the Wealth of Your Lifetime

Many estate planners call the estate tax the voluntary tax. You can give your wealth to the IRS or to your heirs.

But first you have to overcome the widespread myth that you probably do not need an estate plan. Too many people believe myths such as:

- Estate planning and estate taxes are something only the rich worry about.
- Everything will go to my spouse anyway, so I don't need to worry about it.
- Congress repealed the estate tax for middle-income Americans during the 1980s.
- I don't have many assets, so I do not have estate-planning problems.
- I bought life insurance so I wouldn't have to worry about estate taxes.
- My living trust solves all my estate-planning problems.
- My spouse and I own everything jointly; that's all the estate planning we need.
- My assets are worth less than $1.2 million, so I won't have estate-tax problems.

Most of these are myths, half truths, or are based on misinformation. The truth is more like this:

- Everyone needs an estate plan.
- The estate tax was not repealed for middle income Americans.
- A will or a life insurance policy is not an estate plan.
- A living trust solves virtually no estate-tax or income-tax problems.
- Most Americans have much larger taxable estates than they think.

- Leaving everything to your spouse merely defers estate taxes instead of eliminating them.

You do not need to be wealthy to have your family hurt by estate taxes. Federal estate taxes start when the estate value hits $600,000. If your estate is worth $1 million, the estate tax if you do no planning is going to be $153,000. If your estate is worth $2 million, the tax escalates to $588,000.

The estate-tax rate is:

Estate Value	Marginal Rate
$600,001–$750,000	37%
$750,001–1,000,000	39%
$1,000,001–$1,250,000	41%
$1,250,001–1,500,000	43%
$1,500,001–$2,000,000	45%
$2,000,001–$2,500,000	49%
2,500,001–$3,000,000	53%
Over $3,000,000	55%
$10,000,001–$21,040,000	Additional 5%

Also, if you have a large pension or IRA, the "excess" value might be hit with a 15 percent penalty tax. And if you try to avoid estate taxes by putting wealth aside for your grandchildren instead of your children, there is a generation-skipping transfer tax.

The Middle-Class Estate-Tax Trap

Most middle-income and upper-income people do not think of themselves as rich, so they do not think that they have estate-tax or estate-planning problems. But it does not take much to have a $1 million estate these days. A middle-class house is worth $150,000 and up. In many urban and suburban areas the value is substantially higher. Add the value of your cars, household effects, and a modest investment portfolio, and you are getting close to the $600,000 tax-free threshold. If you have a second home, you probably already are well above it. Then there are hidden assets that most people overlook: jointly owned property, life insurance, pensions and IRAs, and inheritances you receive.

Even if you do not have a significant estate-planning problem now, you probably will in a few years. *The estate tax is imposed on the value of your assets at death.* If your house appreciates at the inflation rate, and your investment portfolio appreciates at 8 percent to 10 percent annually, it will not be long before your net worth is well above $1 million.

Let's look at a middle-class couple to show how the estate-tax law is different from what most people think.

Max and Rosie Profits have a typical home for their area; the home is worth about $250,000. They have household effects accumulated over the years, two cars, a modest second home, a small amount of life insurance, Max's pension, and an investment portfolio. They estimate their net worth at about $1.2 million. All their assets are held jointly.

Max and Rosie go to a lawyer who tells them that since their estate is worth only $1.2 million, they will not have an estate-tax problem. He drafts wills in which each spouse leaves all the assets to the other surviving spouse. Let's see what happens if Max dies first.

Max will have a $600,000 estate when he dies, since the property is held jointly. All that property goes to Rosie under his will and the joint property laws. His executor uses the marital deduction to eliminate estate taxes for Max's estate. So far, so good. But Rosie now has a $1.2 million estate and a will that leaves the entire amount to her children. If Rosie dies tomorrow, $600,000 of the estate escapes taxes, but the other $600,000 is fully taxed, for a total tax of $235,000. Almost 20 percent of the Profits' assets will go to the government instead of to their children.

That assumes there is no appreciation. For every dollar that the assets appreciate, the federal government takes more than 40 cents. If the estate appreciates 5 percent annually, it will be worth more than $1.5 million after five years. That increases the estate tax after Rosie's death to at least $363,000.

Bottom line. If you are in your fifties and have assets worth more than $600,000, you might have estate-tax and estate-planning problems. Even if you are older, an estate-tax problem is likely. Most people who are retiring today can look forward to living another twenty or more years. You hope that your assets will increase in value during that time, and if they do, you should take steps to reduce estate taxes.

The Overhyped Living Trust

Many people think they have no estate-planning or estate-tax problems because they have living trusts, perhaps the most promoted estate-planning tool around. But a living trust solves only a couple of estate-planning problems and does nothing to reduce estate or income taxes. It also has some drawbacks.

The traditional living trust is created during your lifetime, and you transfer all your property to the trust. You are trustee and control the property and make transactions just as though you still owned it without the trust. A living trust has these advantages:

- The assets in it avoid probate.
- you have privacy, since the trust is not filed on the public record the way a will is.
- A successor trustee takes over to manage your assets if you become disabled.
- It is more difficult for disgruntled heirs to challenge a living trust than a will.

But a living trust does nothing to reduce income or estate taxes. Under the tax law you are treated as owner of all the trust property; you pay taxes on the income, and the assets are included in your estate.

Another disadvantage of living trusts is that most people do not set them up properly. After getting the trust document, you have to transfer title to all your assets to the trust. That means reregistering cars, changing the deed to your residence, and changing all your financial accounts. If you don't take this step—and many people don't—the living trust doesn't even help you avoid probate. There are many useless living trusts around because trust creators never retitled their assets.

Estate Planning Is More Than Taxes

Most people think that the purpose of estate planning is to avoid taxes, but it is much more. You have to be sure that assets get to the people you intended, that your estate has enough cash to pay expenses, that trusts are properly managed, that someone can take care of your property if you are disabled, that an appropriate guardian for any minor children is appointed, that probate is avoided or costs are minimized, that your business will be properly managed, and that assets are sold or managed by someone who knows about them. Overlooking these important factors is as damaging to many family fortunes as estate taxes.

The Basics of Estate Planning

Your executor compiles a list of all your assets and their values. That is your *gross estate*. Various deductions are subtracted to get your "taxable estate." Your lifetime taxable gifts are added to this, because the estate and gift taxes are considered a uniform wealth transfer tax. It is supposed to cost you the same amount of tax to give money away, whether during your lifetime or at death. Then the executor computes the tax on the sum of your final estate and your lifetime gifts.

After computing the tentative tax, the executor subtracts the gift taxes paid during your lifetime. Then everyone gets an estate- and gift-tax credit of $192,800. That is the equivalent of exempting $600,000 of property from estate taxes. But the credit first is used to reduce gift taxes during your lifetime, and that reduces the credit available to your estate. The estate also gets a credit for state death and inheritance taxes paid.

There are two additional taxes that might be added to the basic estate tax. The excess retirement accumulation tax is an additional tax imposed on pension assets that exceed what Congress decided is a reasonable amount (about $750,000). The generation-skipping tax is imposed when you try to pass assets directly to your grandchildren so that the assets will not be taxed in your children's estate before getting to your grandchildren.

You can see that there is no $600,000 estate-tax exemption. Instead, there is the unified estate- and gift-tax credit, which has the effect of exempting $600,000 of assets. So $600,000 is really known a the "estate-tax exemption equivalent."

You also can see that you have a choice of paying gift taxes now or paying estate taxes later—or using the credit now against gifts instead of later against bequests.

Tax wise estate planning strategies. Now that you know how estate taxes are computed, you can quickly see how estate taxes are reduced. The first strategy for estate-tax reduction is to *reduce your gross estate.* That means either keeping assets out of your estate, or reducing the value of the assets in your estate. Second, *increase the amount of deductions your estate takes. A third strategy is not to worry about reducing estate taxes.* Instead, make sure there are sufficient liquid assets inside or outside the estate to pay the taxes. Often this means buying life insurance through an irrevocable life insurance trust.

Cutting Off the IRS

This chapter gave you an overview of estate planning and an outline of the estate and gift tax. You've seen that the IRS considers you to be richer than you think you are, and it can be dangerous simply to leave all your assets to your spouse. But you can reduce estate taxes by taking valuable property out of your estate, making good use of the marital deduction and charitable deduction, and buying life insurance in some cases. The next chapter shows you specific ways of using these strategies.

Chapter 20

Tax Wise Estate-Planning Strategies

This chapter shows you some specific estate-planning strategies you can use to avoid taxes and preserve wealth for your family.

Strategy 1: Equalize Estate Values of Spouses

A married couple can shield up to $1.2 million of assets from estate taxes—if each spouse takes advantage of his or her $600,000 estate-tax exemption equivalent. That is not possible when one spouse does not have legal title to $600,000 worth of assets, unless they live in a community property state.

Here's a common situation. A couple has $1 million of assets after counting all those hidden assets. But virtually all of the property is in the husband's name. The wife's only legal asset is her joint ownership of their $250,000 home.

If the wife dies first, her estate consists of half of the home's value—$125,000—plus some personal possessions. The estate will get a marital deduction for that amount, resulting in no estate tax due. But the widower now has an estate worth $1 million and only one $600,000 estate-tax exemption equivalent to shield it. That means taxes of $153,000 when he dies unless he does additional estate planning.

The additional taxes could have been avoided and the wife's estate-tax credit would not have been wasted if half the couple's assets had been shifted into the wife's name.

Strategy 2: Maximize Tax-Free Gifts

A key tool in the estate plan of virtually every family is the annual gift-tax exclusion. You can give away up to $10,000 of assets per year to an individual without incurring gift taxes or using up part of your lifetime estate and gift-tax credit. There is no limit to the number of people to whom you can make tax-free gifts each year. A married couple who give jointly can give up to $20,000 gift-tax-free per individual per year.

This is the cheapest and easiest way to reduce estate taxes.

Suppose a couple owns $1.4 million of assets and has two children. They need to give away $200,000 of assets to avoid estate taxes.

Their solution is to give away $20,000 to each child annually. They give away a total of $40,000 per year for five years. After five years their joint estate is down to $1.2 million (assuming no appreciation) and can be passed on estate-tax-free in their wills. They have saved $74,000 of estate taxes.

As their assets appreciate, they can continue giving to their children each year.

When a couple has more substantial assets and has more children and grandchildren, gifts can be made to each child and grandchild. The more offspring or other beneficiaries who are involved, the more property that can be given away tax-free each year.

Naturally, you do not want to let estate taxes dictate what you do with assets. Every couple should retain enough assets to maintain their standard of living and provide for emergencies, even if that might result in estate taxes down the road. But when a couple has more than enough assets and knows who it wants to receive those assets eventually, an annual gifting program is an excellent way to transfer the property now at zero tax cost.

Another advantage of a gifting program is that any income generated by the cash or property that you give away is not taxed to you. You are using the family device to reduce income and estate taxes.

Strategy 3: Protecting Heirs from Themselves

To qualify for the exclusion, a gift must be of a "present interest." Many people do not want to make unrestricted gifts because their children and grandchildren are not old enough or responsible. One way to qualify gifts for the exclusion and not give the heirs complete control of the property is to put the property in an irrevocable trust and give the trust two special provisions: the "Crummey power" and a spendthrift clause.

The trust must be irrevocable, meaning you cannot terminate the trust and get the property back. In addition, neither you nor your spouse can be the trustee. One of your financial advisers can be trustee, an adult child might be, or you can use a bank trust department. The trust must be required to use the income and principal for the needs of the beneficiaries.

The *Crummey* power allows a beneficiary to withdraw the gift from the trust if the request for withdrawal is made during a certain time period after the gift is made, usually thirty days. If the beneficiary does not request a withdrawal, the property stays in the trust under the terms of the trust agreement. The trustee then controls the property and decides how much to distribute to the beneficiaries.

The courts have held that when a trust includes a *Crummey* power, a gift to the trust is a present gift that qualifies for the annual gift-tax exclusion. You can't prevent a beneficiary from exercising the *Crummey* power and demanding the money right away. But if a beneficiary exercises that power one year, you will know not to make any more gifts. Only one year's gifts will be wasted.

The spendthrift clause simply says that the trust property and income cannot be pledged or given as security for the debts of the beneficiaries.

Strategy 4: Give Now Instead of Later

Estate and gift taxes are based on the *value* of assets. If you have assets that appreciate or produce income, they are going to be worth more later than they are now. If you wait to give the property away, the estate taxes in the future will be higher than gift taxes today, or you will use up more of your credit later than you would today. If you do not need an asset to maintain your standard of living and you know who will get it eventually, the family probably will realize a net tax saving by giving the property away sooner rather than later.

Take the case of a successful professional with a net worth of $5 million. He has some investment property worth $300,000. The property has appreciated every year, and all indications are that it will continue to appreciate for years. The professional has no plans to sell the property and plans to leave it to his children.

If he gives the property to his children now he will use up $300,000 of his lifetime estate- and gift-tax exemption equivalent. That will leave $300,000 that he still can give away tax-free either during the rest of his life or in his will.

But if the professional continues to own the property, has a life expectancy of fifteen years, and the property appreciates 5 percent annually, the property would be worth $624,000. That would use all of the estate-tax exemption equivalent. No other assets would be sheltered by the exemption equivalent, and the result will be higher taxes on the entire estate.

If your estate is above the exemption equivalent amount, you should seriously consider giving away appreciating assets now rather than holding them until your death. You want to keep enough assets and liquidity to provide for your foreseeable needs, but consider giving away other assets now.

Another reason to give away property now rather than later is that Congress is continually reviewing proposals to increase estate taxes. It probably is to your benefit to take advantage of the estate- and gift-tax breaks that are available now instead of assuming they will be available in a few years.

Strategy 5: Combining the Marital-Deduction and Estate-Tax Credit

Estate-planning strategies work best when several are used in combination.

Suppose a couple has $1.4 million in assets and uses annual nontaxable gifts to their children to reduce their joint estate to $1.2 million and keep it at that level. They also change legal title of some assets so that each spouse individually owns $600,000 worth.

Their original wills had each spouse leaving all of his or her assets to the other, with everything going to the children if there is no surviving spouse. The consequences of this would be $235,000 in estate taxes. When the first spouse died, no estate taxes would be due because the marital deduction will reduce the taxable estate to zero. But the surviving spouse would own $1.2 million of assets. He or she would be able to shelter only $600,000 from gift or estate taxes. In addition, there would be only one $10,000 annual gift-tax exclusion per donee available to reduce the estate.

An alternative is to change each spouse's will to provide that $600,000 of property would be put in a family trust. The trust would pay income or principal to the surviving spouse for life either under guidelines set in the trust agreement or at the trustee's discretion. After the surviving spouse died, the trust assets would go to the children. The $600,000 in the trust is included in the taxable estate of the first spouse to die but is shielded from taxes by the estate-tax credit. Any remaining assets in the first spouse's estate go to the surviving spouse, so they are shielded from taxes by the marital deduction.

The result is no estate taxes on the death of the first spouse to die. The surviving spouse still has the benefit of the assets in the trust, but they will not be included in his or her estate. And the $600,000 of assets retained by the surviving spouse will pass to the children or other heirs because of that spouse's estate-tax credit.

This arrangement has several names: the credit shelter trust, A-B trust, family trust, and bypass trust. This is the most common arrangement for middle-income couples and can save substantial wealth for your heirs.

In some states a better alternative is the pour-over trust. The effect is the same. The difference is that you create a revocable trust during your lifetime and provide in your will that $600,000 of assets will be transferred to the trust after your death. Which strategy you use depends on the state in which you live; you should consult a local estate planner to devise your plan.

Strategy 6: Protecting Assets and Heirs with QTip Trust

Suppose you are married and want to leave the bulk of these assets to your spouse in your will. But you have a couple of concerns. One is that your spouse is not financially sophisticated and might not manage the assets well after your death. The other concern is to ensure that the assets do not go to a second spouse or the children of a second spouse if your spouse should remarry. Or you might not want the assets to go to the children of your spouse's marriage before you two were married.

You can provide for your spouse and eliminate these concerns by using a QTIP trust.

Instead of leaving the assets outright to your spouse, you leave the assets to a QTIP trust. The trust provides that the spouse will get all income from the trust for life and might be able to get some principal from the trust under certain circumstances. After the spouse dies, the remaining trust property is distributed as directed in the trust agreement.

The property placed in the QTIP trust qualifies for the marital deduction. The property in the QTIP trust will be included in the estate of your spouse. So the trust will use up the second spouse's estate-tax credit, or there must be enough liquid assets or insurance available to the estate to pay the taxes.

There are a number of technical provisions that must be complied with to qualify the QTIP trust for the marital deduction. Be sure you have an estate planner who is familiar with this type of trust if you want to explore this strategy.

Strategy 7: Deciding to Let Uncle Sam Get His Share

Sometimes the traditional estate-planning strategies are not practical. For example, it can be difficult to give away real estate over the years in $10,000 increments. Or you might not want to put your business interests in a trust. In these and other cases you might decide not to look for ways to *reduce* estate taxes. Instead, you decide to let life insurance *pay* the taxes.

Let's look at the case of Max and Rosie Profits. Max's business is worth $5 million. Giving away shares of the business now is not acceptable to Max.

So instead of planning to remove the business from his estate, Max decides to retain ownership of the business, estimates the maximum tax the estate will have to pay, and buys life insurance to cover this tax bill. But there is an additional step Max must take to get the maximum benefit of this strategy.

Life insurance will be included in Max's estate when he has any "incidents of ownership" over the policy. Or if Max buys a policy and names his estate as the beneficiary, then the insurance proceeds will be part of his estate and subject to estate taxes. That means Max will have to buy even more life insurance to pay the additional estate taxes on the life insurance.

A better solution is for Max to set up an irrevocable life insurance trust. The trust has an independent trustee who is empowered to buy insurance on Max's life. The trust agreement provides that any insurance benefits will be paid to Max's estaste to pay the taxes and other expenses. Any additional amounts will be paid to other beneficiaries designated by Max. Max transfers money to the trust each year to pay insurance premiums.

The result is that Max's business and other assets stay intact and the estate taxes are fully paid.

A life insurance policy can meet estate planning needs whenever an estate is composed of assets that cannot be divided through gifts or other means over years, or when the assets are illiquid and you do not want to risk having them sold at fire-sale prices after your death. Ideal users of this strategy are those owning businesses, real estate, collectibles, or investments that are illiquid or highly volatile.

Instead of reducing the estate-tax bill, you are agreeing to pay the full tax but are looking for a way to pay it at a discount.

Strategy 8: Getting Maximum Insurance Benefits for the Dollar

Life insurance can be expensive. One way for a married couple to drive down the cost while using insurance to pay estate taxes is to use a type of life insurance known as second-to-die or survivorship life insurance.

The policy pays only after both spouses have died. Since two lives are being insured rather than one, the insurance is cheaper per dollar of benefits than a single life policy. But survivorship policies are fairly tricky, and the policy that seems cheapest at first can turn out to be more expensive over time.

Most survivorship policies have a "vanishing premium" feature. You pay premiums for a period of years, usually seven; then the insurance is paid up for the rest of both your lives.

But that is mostly theory. The vanishing date of the premiums is not guaranteed; it is based on estimates. Part of each of your premiums pays for life insurance; the remainder goes into a cash value account. The cash value account is assumed to earn enough income to pay the future premiums. If the account earns less income than projected, you will have to pay additional premiums in the future or let the policy lapse.

When someone shows you projections that have the premiums vanishing, find out the interest rate that is assumed. If it is based on earnings from the 1980s or early 1990s, it probably is unrealistic.

There also are some clauses you need to consider in a survivorship policy.

Since insurers do not have much experience with survivorship policies, some insurers insert a clause that allows them to increase premiums in ten or fifteen years. Some insurers are even allowed to double premiums down the road if expectations are not met. You can buy survivorship insurance without this provision, and you probably should. You do not want to get hit with a premium increase when you are in your seventies or eighties.

Some insurers also retain the right to increase premiums if one spouse dies within a year or two after the policy is issued. The insurers say that an early death drastically alters their assumptions. But you can get a policy without this clause and should do so.

You want a policy that allows you to split the policy into two separate policies without new evidence of insurability in the case of a divorce. Another good feature allows you to increase the death benefit without additional evidence of insurability. This is protection against your estate growing faster than you anticipate or your living much longer than expected.

You also want a tax law change clause. This allows you to surrender the policy for the return of 100 percent of premiums paid if the tax law changes adversely within a year after you purchase the policy.

It is especially important that you compare survivorship policies from different insurers. Premiums vary considerably for essentially the same policy. It is not unusual for one insurer to offer the best premiums for one age level but relatively high premiums at another age level.

Strategy 9: Passing On the Home for Maximum Tax Advantage

For many families, the home is one of the most valuable assets. One of the trickiest aspects of estate planning is transferring the family residence while incurring a minimum of estate or gift taxes.

One useful strategy is the personal residence trust. You put the house in a trust for a fixed period of years. The trust agreement allows you to live in the home for the period of the trust. After that, the home belongs to the trust beneficiaries. In most cases the trustees and the beneficiaries are your children. You can continue to live in the home after the trust period, but you have to pay rent to the children, or they have to treat the rental value as a gift.

With this trust, a taxable gift to the trust beneficiaries occurs at the time the trust is created. The gift is less than the full value of the house; it is the value of the remainder interest of the trust beneficiaries and is determined by IRS tables that take into account your age, the value of the home, and current interest rates. The house and its appreciation then are out of your estate. The drawback to this strategy is that if you die before the trust period ends, the entire value of the house is included in your gross estate and the strategy has no effect.

Many people feel uneasy using the personal residence trust for their primary residence. They want to own their homes for the rest of their lives. But the personal residence trust sometimes is used effectively for second homes without the insecurity and other problems that come from using the strategy for a primary residence.

Strategy 10: Profit by Giving Assets Away

Creative charitable giving strategies are excellent ways to reduce both income and estate taxes. Your estate gets a deduction for any charitable gifts made with your assets. That means those assets are not taxed.

Many of the strategies described in the charitable giving chapter work for estate plans as well as for income-tax plans. You can provide for your heirs and reduce estate taxes by giving a charity a remainder interest in your home or other property, by setting up charitable remainder or charitable lead trusts, or by setting up a private foundation. If you want to provide for both your heirs and for charity, consider these strategies.

Strategy 11: Preserving Assets with the Family Limited Partnership

A strategy that is becoming very popular for people with substantial investment assets or small businesses is the family limited partnership. The partnership allows you to retain significant control over property while giving it away to your family at a reduced tax cost.

You form a partnership with yourself and possibly your spouse as general partners having a 1 percent ownership interest. Then you transfer property into the partnership in exchange for the limited partnership interests. You can give or sell the limited partnership interests to your children and grandchildren either at one time or over a period of years.

One advantage of this strategy is that the general partner usually determines how the partnership property is managed. You can control the assets and decide how much income is distributed. In addition, each partner does not have to receive equal distributions. You can make cash distributions as you think each child needs the money. But each partner will be taxed on his or her proportionate share of the income, whether or not it is distributed. So the partnership helps split income among family members, who might be in lower tax brackets. You could, for example, distribute just enough cash to help the partners pay their income taxes on the partnership income, then leave the rest of the cash in the partnership.

But the big advantage of the family limited partnership is that you get a gift tax discount. Remember that you pay gift taxes on the value of the property you give to your children. But when you give away business interests, an interest of less than 50 percent gets a minority discount, because a minority interest in a small business is worth less than its proportionate share of the business's total value. Minority discounts typically are 20 percent to 40 percent, though some cases have allowed discounts of up to 60 percent. The family limited partnership lets you pay gift taxes at a discount of 20 percent to 60 percent of what the estate taxes would have been.

Strategy 12: Giving Property Away, but Keeping the Income and Cutting Taxes

Sometimes you want to get some property out of your estate but want to keep the income from the property. One effective way to accomplish your goals, especially with appreciating property, is to establish a grantor-retained-income trust (GRIT).

The GRIT pays you income for life or a period of years. Then the trust terminates, and other beneficiaries you designated get the property. You pay a gift tax or use your lifetime estate and gift tax credit when the trust is established, but the gift is the value of the property minus the present value of the income stream you will receive. So the property is out of your estate at a reduced tax cost.

The potential disadvantage is that if you outlive the trust term, you no longer receive the income.

You probably do not want to use a GRIT with appreciated property that you or your children would sell. The GRIT will be taxed on the capital gains from the sale of its assets. You do not avoid those taxes by transferring the property to the trust or letting your children get it through the trust. But a GRIT is good for income-producing securities that you plan to leave for your children.

GRITs come in two varieties: grantor-retained-annuity trusts (GRATs) and grantor-retained unitrusts (GRUTs). The difference is that the GRAT pays you a fixed dollar amount each year, while the GRUT pays a fixed percentage of the trust's value each year.